AI Innovations and Self-Driving Cars

Practical Advances in Artificial Intelligence (AI)
and Machine Learning

Dr. Lance B. Eliot, MBA, PhD

DEDICATION

To my incredible son, Michael, and my incredible daughter, Lauren.

Forest fortuna adiuvat (from the Latin; good fortune favors the brave).

CONTENTS

Lance B. Eliot

ACKNOWLEDGMENTS

I have been the beneficiary of advice and counsel by many friends, colleagues, family, investors, and many others. I want to thank everyone that has aided me throughout my career. I write from the heart and the head, having experienced first-hand what it means to have others around you that support you during the good times and the tough times.

To Warren Bennis, one of my doctoral advisors and ultimately a colleague, I offer my deepest thanks and appreciation, especially for his calm and insightful wisdom and support.

To Mark Stevens and his generous efforts toward funding and supporting the USC Stevens Center for Innovation.

To Lloyd Greif and the USC Lloyd Greif Center for Entrepreneurial Studies for their ongoing encouragement of founders and entrepreneurs.

To Peter Drucker, William Wang, Aaron Levie, Peter Kim, Jon Kraft, Cindy Crawford, Jenny Ming, Steve Milligan, Chis Underwood, Frank Gehry, Buzz Aldrin, Steve Forbes, Bill Thompson, Dave Dillon, Alan Fuerstman, Larry Ellison, Jim Sinegal, John Sperling, Mark Stevenson, Anand Nallathambi, Thomas Barrack, Jr., and many other innovators and leaders that I have met and gained mightily from doing so.

Thanks to Ed Trainor, Kevin Anderson, James Hickey, Wendell Jones, Ken Harris, DuWayne Peterson, Mike Brown, Jim Thornton, Abhi Beniwal, Al Biland, John Nomura, Eliot Weinman, John Desmond, and many others for their unwavering support during my career.

And most of all thanks as always to Lauren and Michael, for their ongoing support and for having seen me writing and heard much of this material during the many months involved in writing it. To their patience and willingness to listen.

INTRODUCTION

This is a book that provides the newest innovations and the latest Artificial Intelligence (AI) advances about the emerging nature of AI-based autonomous self-driving driverless cars. Via recent advances in Artificial Intelligence (AI) and Machine Learning (ML), we are nearing the day when vehicles can control themselves and will not require and nor rely upon human intervention to perform their driving tasks (or, that <u>allow</u> for human intervention, but only *require* human intervention in very limited ways).

Similar to my other related books, which I describe in a moment and list the chapters in the Appendix A of this book, I am particularly focused on those advances that pertain to self-driving cars. The phrase "autonomous vehicles" is often used to refer to any kind of vehicle, whether it is ground-based or in the air or sea, and whether it is a cargo hauling trailer truck or a conventional passenger car. Though the aspects described in this book are certainly applicable to all kinds of autonomous vehicles, I am focused more so here on cars.

Indeed, I am especially known for my role in aiding the advancement of self-driving cars, serving currently as the Executive Director of the Cybernetic Self-Driving Cars Institute.. In addition to writing software, designing and developing systems and software for self-driving cars, I also speak and write quite a bit about the topic. This book is a collection of some of my more advanced essays. For those of you that might have seen my essays posted elsewhere, I have updated them and integrated them into this book as one handy cohesive package.

You might be interested in companion books that I have written that provide additional key innovations and fundamentals about self-driving cars. Those books are entitled **"Introduction to Driverless Self-Driving Cars,"** "Advances in AI and Autonomous Vehicles: Cybernetic Self-Driving Cars," "Self-Driving Cars: "The Mother of All AI Projects," "Innovation and Thought Leadership on Self-Driving Driverless Cars," "New Advances in AI Autonomous Driverless Self-Driving Cars," and "Autonomous Vehicle Driverless Self-Driving Cars and

Artificial Intelligence" and **"Transformative Artificial Intelligence Driverless Self-Driving Cars,"** and **"Disruptive Artificial Intelligence and Driverless Self-Driving Cars,** and **"State-of-the-Art AI Driverless Self-Driving Cars"** and **"Top Trends in AI Self-Driving Cars"** (they are all available via Amazon). See Appendix A of this herein book to see a listing of the chapters covered in those three books.

For the introduction here to this book, I am going to borrow my introduction from those companion books, since it does a good job of laying out the landscape of self-driving cars and my overall viewpoints on the topic. The remainder of the book is all new material that does not appear in the companion books.

INTRODUCTION TO SELF-DRIVING CARS

This is a book about self-driving cars. Someday in the future, we'll all have self-driving cars and this book will perhaps seem antiquated, but right now, we are at the forefront of the self-driving car wave. Daily news bombards us with flashes of new announcements by one car maker or another and leaves the impression that within the next few weeks or maybe months that the self-driving car will be here. A casual non-technical reader would assume from these news flashes that in fact we must be on the cusp of a true self-driving car.

Here's a real news flash: We are still quite a distance from having a true self-driving car. It is years to go before we get there.

Why is that? Because a true self-driving car is akin to a moonshot. In the same manner that getting us to the moon was an incredible feat, likewise can it be said for achieving a true self-driving car. Anybody that suggests or even brashly states that the true self-driving car is nearly here should be viewed with great skepticism. Indeed, you'll see that I often tend to use the word "hogwash" or "crock" when I assess much of the decidedly *fake news* about self-driving cars. Those of us on the inside know that what is often reported to the outside is malarkey. Few of the insiders are willing to say so. I have no such hesitation.

Indeed, I've been writing a popular blog post about self-driving cars and hitting hard on those that try to wave their hands and pretend that we are on the imminent verge of true self-driving cars. For many years, I've been known as the AI Insider. Besides writing about AI, I also develop AI software. I do what I describe. It also gives me insights into what others that are doing AI are really doing versus what it is said they are doing.

Many faithful readers had asked me to pull together my insightful short essays and put them into another book, which you are now holding in your hands.

For those of you that have been reading my essays over the years, this collection not only puts them together into one handy package, I also updated the essays and added new material. For those of you that are new to the topic of self-driving cars and AI, I hope you find these essays approachable and informative. I also tend to have a writing style with a bit of a voice, and so you'll see that I am times have a wry sense of humor and also like to poke at conformity.

As a former professor and founder of an AI research lab, I for many years wrote in the formal language of academic writing. I published in referred journals and served as an editor for several AI journals. This writing here is not of the nature, and I have adopted a different and more informal style for these essays. That being said, I also do mention from time-to-time more rigorous material on AI and encourage you all to dig into those deeper and more formal materials if so interested.

I am also an AI practitioner. This means that I write AI software for a living. Currently, I head-up the Cybernetics Self-Driving Car Institute, where we are developing AI software for self-driving cars. I am excited to also report that my son, also a software engineer, heads-up our Cybernetics Self-Driving Car Lab. What I have helped to start, and for which he is an integral part, ultimately he will carry long into the future after I have retired. My daughter, a marketing whiz, also is integral to our efforts as head of our Marketing group. She too will carry forward the legacy now being formulated.

For those of you that are reading this book and have a penchant for writing code, you might consider taking a look at the open source code available for self-driving cars. This is a handy place to start learning how to develop AI for self-driving cars. There are also many new educational courses spring forth.

There is a growing body of those wanting to learn about and develop self-driving cars, and a growing body of colleges, labs, and other avenues by which you can learn about self-driving cars.

This book will provide a foundation of aspects that I think will get you ready for those kinds of more advanced training opportunities. If you've already taken those classes, you'll likely find these essays especially interesting as they offer a perspective that I am betting few other instructors or faculty offered to you. These are challenging essays that ask you to think beyond the conventional about self-driving cars.

THE MOTHER OF ALL AI PROJECTS

In June 2017, Apple CEO Tim Cook came out and finally admitted that Apple has been working on a self-driving car. As you'll see in my essays,

Apple was enmeshed in secrecy about their self-driving car efforts. We have only been able to read the tea leaves and guess at what Apple has been up to. The notion of an iCar has been floating for quite a while, and self-driving engineers and researchers have been signing tight-lipped Non-Disclosure Agreements (NDA's) to work on projects at Apple that were as shrouded in mystery as any military invasion plans might be.

Tim Cook said something that many others in the Artificial Intelligence (AI) field have been saying, namely, the creation of a self-driving car has got to be the mother of all AI projects. In other words, it is in fact a tremendous moonshot for AI. If a self-driving car can be crafted and the AI works as we hope, it means that we have made incredible strides with AI and that therefore it opens many other worlds of potential breakthrough accomplishments that AI can solve.

Is this hyperbole? Am I just trying to make AI seem like a miracle worker and so provide self-aggrandizing statements for those of us writing the AI software for self-driving cars? No, it is not hyperbole. Developing a true self-driving car is really, really, really hard to do. Let me take a moment to explain why. As a side note, I realize that the Apple CEO is known for at times uttering hyperbole, and he had previously said for example that the year 2012 was "the mother of all years," and he had said that the release of iOS 10 was "the mother of all releases" – all of which does suggest he likes to use the handy "mother of" expression. But, I assure you, in terms of true self-driving cars, he has hit the nail on the head. For sure.

When you think about a moonshot and how we got to the moon, there are some identifiable characteristics and those same aspects can be applied to creating a true self-driving car. You'll notice that I keep putting the word "true" in front of the self-driving car expression. I do so because as per my essay about the various levels of self-driving cars, there are some self-driving cars that are only somewhat of a self-driving car. The somewhat versions are ones that require a human driver to be ready to intervene. In my view, that's not a true self-driving car. A true self-driving car is one that requires no human driver intervention at all. It is a car that can entirely undertake via automation the driving task without any human driver needed. This is the essence of what is known as a Level 5 self-driving car. We are currently at the Level 2 and Level 3 mark, and not yet at Level 5.

Getting to the moon involved aspects such as having big stretch goals, incremental progress, experimentation, innovation, and so on. Let's review how this applied to the moonshot of the bygone era, and how it applies to the self-driving car moonshot of today.

Big Stretch Goal

Trying to take a human and deliver the human to the moon, and bring them back, safely, was an extremely large stretch goal at the time. No one knew whether it could be done. The technology wasn't available yet. The cost was huge. The determination would need to be fierce. Etc. To reach a Level 5 self-driving car is going to be the same. It is a big stretch goal. We can readily get to the Level 3, and we are able to see the Level 4 just up ahead, but a Level 5 is still an unknown as to if it is doable. It should eventually be doable and in the same way that we thought we'd eventually get to the moon, but when it will occur is a different story.

Incremental Progress

Getting to the moon did not happen overnight in one fell swoop. It took years and years of incremental progress to get there. Likewise for self-driving cars. Google has famously been striving to get to the Level 5, and pretty much been willing to forgo dealing with the intervening levels, but most of the other self-driving car makers are doing the incremental route. Let's get a good Level 2 and a somewhat Level 3 going. Then, let's improve the Level 3 and get a somewhat Level 4 going. Then, let's improve the Level 4 and finally arrive at a Level 5. This seems to be the prevalent way that we are going to achieve the true self-driving car.

Experimentation

You likely know that there were various experiments involved in perfecting the approach and technology to get to the moon. As per making incremental progress, we first tried to see if we could get a rocket to go into space and safety return, then put a monkey in there, then with a human, then we went all the way to the moon but didn't land, and finally we arrived at the mission that actually landed on the moon. Self-driving cars are the same way. We are doing simulations of self-driving cars. We do testing of self-driving cars on private land under controlled situations. We do testing of self-driving cars on public roadways, often having to meet regulatory requirements including for example having an engineer or equivalent in the car to take over the controls if needed. And so on. Experiments big and small are needed to figure out what works and what doesn't.

Innovation

There are already some advances in AI that are allowing us to progress toward self-driving cars. We are going to need even more advances. Innovation in all aspects of technology are going to be required to achieve a true self-driving car. By no means do we already have everything in-hand that we need to get there. Expect new inventions and new approaches, new algorithms, etc.

Setbacks

Most of the pundits are avoiding talking about potential setbacks in the progress toward self-driving cars. Getting to the moon involved many setbacks, some of which you never have heard of and were buried at the time so as to not dampen enthusiasm and funding for getting to the moon. A recurring theme in many of my included essays is that there are going to be setbacks as we try to arrive at a true self-driving car. Take a deep breath and be ready. I just hope the setbacks don't completely stop progress. I am sure that it will cause progress to alter in a manner that we've not yet seen in the self-driving car field. I liken the self-driving car of today to the excitement everyone had for Uber when it first got going. Today, we have a different view of Uber and with each passing day there are more regulations to the ride sharing business and more concerns raised. The darling child only stays a darling until finally that child acts up. It will happen the same with self-driving cars.

SELF-DRIVING CARS CHALLENGES

But what exactly makes things so hard to have a true self-driving car, you might be asking. You have seen cruise control for years and years. You've lately seen cars that can do parallel parking. You've seen YouTube videos of Tesla drivers that put their hands out the window as their car zooms along the highway, and seen to therefore be in a self-driving car. Aren't we just needing to put a few more sensors onto a car and then we'll have in-hand a true self-driving car? Nope.

Consider for a moment the nature of the driving task. We don't just let anyone at any age drive a car. Worldwide, most countries won't license a driver until the age of 18, though many do allow a learner's permit at the age of 15 or 16. Some suggest that a younger age would be physically too small to reach the controls of the car. Though this might be the case, we could easily adjust the controls to allow for younger aged and thus smaller stature. It's not their physical size that matters. It's their cognitive development that matters.

To drive a car, you need to be able to reason about the car, what the car can and cannot do. You need to know how to operate the car. You need to know about how other cars on the road drive. You need to know what is allowed in driving such as speed limits and driving within marked lanes. You need to be able to react to situations and be able to avoid getting into accidents. You need to ascertain when to hit your brakes, when to steer clear of a pedestrian, and how to keep from ramming that motorcyclist that just cut you off.

Many of us had taken courses on driving. We studied about driving and took driver training. We had to take a test and pass it to be able to drive. The point being that though most adults take the driving task for granted, and we often "mindlessly" drive our cars, there is a significant amount of cognitive effort that goes into driving a car. After a while, it becomes second nature. You don't especially think about how you drive, you just do it. But, if you watch a novice driver, say a teenager learning to drive, you suddenly realize that there is a lot more complexity to it than we seem to realize.

Furthermore, driving is a very serious task. I recall when my daughter and son first learned to drive. They are both very conscientious people. They wanted to make sure that whatever they did, they did well, and that they did not harm anyone. Every day, when you get into a car, it is probably around 4,000 pounds of hefty metal and plastics (about two tons), and it is a lethal weapon. Think about it. You drive down the street in an object that weighs two tons and with the engine it can accelerate and ram into anything you want to hit. The damage a car can inflict is very scary. Both my children were surprised that they were being given the right to maneuver this monster of a beast that could cause tremendous harm entirely by merely letting go of the steering wheel for a moment or taking your eyes off the road.

In fact, in the United States alone there are about 30,000 deaths per year by auto accidents, which is around 100 per day. Given that there are about 263 million cars in the United States, I am actually more amazed that the number of fatalities is not a lot higher. During my morning commute, I look at all the thousands of cars on the freeway around me, and I think that if all of them decided to go zombie and drive in a crazy maniac way, there would be many people dead. Somehow, incredibly, each day, most people drive relatively safely. To me, that's a miracle right there. Getting millions and millions of people to be safe and sane when behind the wheel of a two ton mobile object, it's a feat that we as a society should admire with pride.

So, hopefully you are in agreement that the driving task requires a great deal of cognition. You don't' need to be especially smart to drive a car, and we've done quite a bit to make car driving viable for even the average dolt. There isn't an IQ test that you need to take to drive a car. If you can read and write, and pass a test, you pretty much can legally drive a car. There are of course some that drive a car and are not legally permitted to do so, plus there are private areas such as farms where drivers are young, but for public roadways in the United States, you can be generally of average intelligence (or less) and be able to legally drive.

This though makes it seem like the cognitive effort must not be much. If the cognitive effort was truly hard, wouldn't we only have Einstein's that could drive a car? We have made sure to keep the driving task as simple as we can, by making the controls easy and relatively standardized, and by having roads that are relatively standardized, and so on. It is as though Disneyland has put their Autopia into the real-world, by us all as a society agreeing that roads will be a certain way, and we'll all abide by the various rules of driving.

A modest cognitive task by a human is still something that stymies AI. You certainly know that AI has been able to beat chess players and be good at other kinds of games. This type of narrow cognition is not what car driving is about. Car driving is much wider. It requires knowledge about the world, which a chess playing AI system does not need to know. The cognitive aspects of driving are on the one hand seemingly simple, but at the same time require layer upon layer of knowledge about cars, people, roads, rules, and a myriad of other "common sense" aspects. We don't have any AI systems today that have that same kind of breadth and depth of awareness and knowledge.

As revealed in my essays, the self-driving car of today is using trickery to do particular tasks. It is all very narrow in operation. Plus, it currently assumes that a human driver is ready to intervene. It is like a child that we have taught to stack blocks, but we are needed to be right there in case the child stacks them too high and they begin to fall over. AI of today is brittle, it is narrow, and it does not approach the cognitive abilities of humans. This is why the true self-driving car is somewhere out in the future.

Another aspect to the driving task is that it is not solely a mind exercise. You do need to use your senses to drive. You use your eyes a vision sensors to see the road ahead. You vision capability is like a streaming video, which your brain needs to continually analyze as you drive. Where is the road? Is there a pedestrian in the way? Is there another car ahead of you? Your senses are relying a flood of info to your brain. Self-driving cars are trying to do the same, by using cameras, radar, ultrasound, and lasers. This is an attempt at mimicking how humans have senses and sensory apparatus.

Thus, the driving task is mental and physical. You use your senses, you use your arms and legs to manipulate the controls of the car, and you use your brain to assess the sensory info and direct your limbs to act upon the controls of the car. This all happens instantly. If you've ever perhaps gotten something in your eye and only had one eye available to drive with, you suddenly realize how dependent upon vision you are. If you have a broken foot with a cast, you suddenly realize how hard it is to control the brake pedal and the accelerator. If you've taken medication and your brain is maybe sluggish, you suddenly realize how much mental strain is required to drive a car.

An AI system that plays chess only needs to be focused on playing chess.

The physical aspects aren't important because usually a human moves the chess pieces or the chessboard is shown on an electronic display. Using AI for a more life-and-death task such as analyzing MRI images of patients, this again does not require physical capabilities and instead is done by examining images of bits.

Driving a car is a true life-and-death task. It is a use of AI that can easily and at any moment produce death. For those colleagues of mine that are developing this AI, as am I, we need to keep in mind the somber aspects of this. We are producing software that will have in its virtual hands the lives of the occupants of the car, and the lives of those in other nearby cars, and the lives of nearby pedestrians, etc. Chess is not usually a life-or-death matter.

Driving is all around us. Cars are everywhere. Most of today's AI applications involve only a small number of people. Or, they are behind the scenes and we as humans have other recourse if the AI messes up. AI that is driving a car at 80 miles per hour on a highway had better not mess up. The consequences are grave. Multiply this by the number of cars, if we could put magically self-driving into every car in the USA, we'd have AI running in the 263 million cars. That's a lot of AI spread around. This is AI on a massive scale that we are not doing today and that offers both promise and potential peril.

There are some that want AI for self-driving cars because they envision a world without any car accidents. They envision a world in which there is no car congestion and all cars cooperate with each other. These are wonderful utopian visions.

They are also very misleading. The adoption of self-driving cars is going to be incremental and not overnight. We cannot economically just junk all existing cars. Nor are we going to be able to affordably retrofit existing cars. It is more likely that self-driving cars will be built into new cars and that over many years of gradual replacement of existing cars that we'll see the mix of self-driving cars become substantial in the real-world.

In these essays, I have tried to offer technological insights without being overly technical in my description, and also blended the business, societal, and economic aspects too. Technologists need to consider the non-technological impacts of what they do. Non-technologists should be aware of what is being developed.

We all need to work together to collectively be prepared for the enormous disruption and transformative aspects of true self-driving cars. We all need to be involved in this mother of all AI projects.

WHAT THIS BOOK PROVIDES

What does this book provide to you? It introduces many of the key elements about self-driving cars and does so with an AI based perspective. I weave together technical and non-technical aspects, readily going from being concerned about the cognitive capabilities of the driving task and how the technology is embodying this into self-driving cars, and in the next breath I discuss the societal and economic aspects.

They are all intertwined because that's the way reality is. You cannot separate out the technology per se, and instead must consider it within the milieu of what is being invented and innovated, and do so with a mindset towards the contemporary mores and culture that shape what we are doing and what we hope to do.

WHY THIS BOOK

I wrote this book to try and bring to the public view many aspects about self-driving cars that nobody seems to be discussing.

For business leaders that are either involved in making self-driving cars or that are going to leverage self-driving cars, I hope that this book will enlighten you as to the risks involved and ways in which you should be strategizing about how to deal with those risks.

For entrepreneurs, startups and other businesses that want to enter into the self-driving car market that is emerging, I hope this book sparks your interest in doing so, and provides some sense of what might be prudent to pursue.

For researchers that study self-driving cars, I hope this book spurs your interest in the risks and safety issues of self-driving cars, and also nudges you toward conducting research on those aspects.

For students in computer science or related disciplines, I hope this book will provide you with interesting and new ideas and material, for which you might conduct research or provide some career direction insights for you.

For AI companies and high-tech companies pursuing self-driving cars, this book will hopefully broaden your view beyond just the mere coding and development needed to make self-driving cars.

For all readers, I hope that you will find the material in this book to be stimulating. Some of it will be repetitive of things you already know. But I am pretty sure that you'll also find various eureka moments whereby you'll discover a new technique or approach that you had not earlier thought of. I am also betting that there will be material that forces you to rethink some of your current practices.

I am not saying you will suddenly have an epiphany and change what you are doing. I do think though that you will reconsider or perhaps revisit what you are doing.

For anyone choosing to use this book for teaching purposes, please take a look at my suggestions for doing so, as described in the Appendix. I have found the material handy in courses that I have taught, and likewise other faculty have told me that they have found the material handy, in some cases as extended readings and in other instances as a core part of their course (depending on the nature of the class).

In my writing for this book, I have tried carefully to blend both the practitioner and the academic styles of writing. It is not as dense as is typical academic journal writing, but at the same time offers depth by going into the nuances and trade-offs of various practices.

The word "deep" is in vogue today, meaning getting deeply into a subject or topic, and so is the word "unpack" which means to tease out the underlying aspects of a subject or topic. I have sought to offer material that addresses an issue or topic by going relatively deeply into it and make sure that it is well unpacked.

Finally, in any book about AI, it is difficult to use our everyday words without having some of them be misinterpreted. Specifically, it is easy to anthropomorphize AI. When I say that an AI system "knows" something, I do not want you to construe that the AI system has sentience and "knows" in the same way that humans do. They aren't that way, as yet. I have tried to use quotes around such words from time-to-time to emphasize that the words I am using should not be misinterpreted to ascribe true human intelligence to the AI systems that we know of today. If I used quotes around all such words, the book would be very difficult to read, and so I am doing so judiciously. Please keep that in mind as you read the material, thanks.

COMPANION BOOKS

If you find this material of interest, you might want to also see my other books on self-driving cars, entitled:

1. **"Introduction to Driverless Self-Driving Cars"** by Dr. Lance Eliot

2. **"Innovation and Thought Leadership on Self-Driving Driverless Cars"** by Dr. Lance Eliot

3. **"Advances in AI and Autonomous Vehicles: Cybernetic Self-Driving Cars"** by Dr. Lance Eliot

4. ***"Self-Driving Cars: The Mother of All AI Projects"*** by Dr. Lance Eliot

5. **"New Advances in AI Autonomous Driverless Self-Driving Cars"** by Dr. Lance Eliot

6. **"Autonomous Vehicle Driverless Self-Driving Cars and Artificial Intelligence"** by Dr. Lance Eliot and Michael B. Eliot

7. **"Transformative Artificial Intelligence Driverless Self-Driving Cars"** by Dr. Lance Eliot

8. **"Disruptive Artificial Intelligence and Driverless Self-Driving Cars"** by Dr. Lance Eliot

9. **"State-of-the-Art AI Driverless Self-Driving Cars"** by Dr. Lance Eliot

10. **"Top Trends in AI Self-Driving Cars"** by Dr. Lance Eliot

11. **"AI Innovations and Self-Driving Cars"** by Dr. Lance Eliot

All of the above books are available on Amazon and at other major global booksellers.

CHAPTER 1

ELIOT FRAMEWORK FOR AI SELF-DRIVING CARS

CHAPTER 1

ELIOT FRAMEWORK FOR AI SELF-DRIVING CARS

This chapter is a core foundational aspect for understanding AI self-driving cars and I have used this same chapter in several of my other books to introduce the reader to essential elements of this field. Once you've read this chapter, you'll be prepared to read the rest of the material since the foundational essence of the components of autonomous AI driverless self-driving cars will have been established for you.

When I give presentations about self-driving cars and teach classes on the topic, I have found it helpful to provide a framework around which the various key elements of self-driving cars can be understood and organized (see diagram at the end of this chapter). The framework needs to be simple enough to convey the overarching elements, but at the same time not so simple that it belies the true complexity of self-driving cars. As such, I am going to describe the framework here and try to offer in a thousand words (or more!) what the framework diagram itself intends to portray.

The core elements on the diagram are numbered for ease of reference. The numbering does not suggest any kind of prioritization of the elements. Each element is crucial. Each element has a purpose, and otherwise would not be included in the framework. For some self-driving cars, a particular element might be more important or somehow distinguished in comparison to other self-driving cars.

You could even use the framework to rate a particular self-driving car, doing so by gauging how well it performs in each of the elements of the framework. I will describe each of the elements, one at a time. After doing so, I'll discuss aspects that illustrate how the elements interact and perform during the overall effort of a self-driving car.

At the Cybernetic Self-Driving Car Institute, we use the framework to keep track of what we are working on, and how we are developing software that fills in what is needed to achieve Level 5 self-driving cars.

D-01: Sensor Capture

Let's start with the one element that often gets the most attention in the press about self-driving cars, namely, the sensory devices for a self-driving car.

On the framework, the box labeled as D-01 indicates "Sensor Capture" and refers to the processes of the self-driving car that involve collecting data from the myriad of sensors that are used for a self-driving car. The types of devices typically involved are listed, such as the use of mono cameras, stereo cameras, LIDAR devices, radar systems, ultrasonic devices, GPS, IMU, and so on.

These devices are tasked with obtaining data about the status of the self-driving car and the world around it. Some of the devices are continually providing updates, while others of the devices await an indication by the self-driving car that the device is supposed to collect data. The data might be first transformed in some fashion by the device itself, or it might instead be fed directly into the sensor capture as raw data. At that point, it might be up to the sensor capture processes to do transformations on the data. This all varies depending upon the nature of the devices being used and how the devices were designed and developed.

D-02: Sensor Fusion

Imagine that your eyeballs receive visual images, your nose receives odors, your ears receive sounds, and in essence each of your distinct sensory devices is getting some form of input. The input befits the nature of the device. Likewise, for a self-driving car, the cameras provide visual images, the radar returns radar reflections, and so on.

Each device provides the data as befits what the device does.

At some point, using the analogy to humans, you need to merge together what your eyes see, what your nose smells, what your ears hear, and piece it all together into a larger sense of what the world is all about and what is happening around you. Sensor fusion is the action of taking the singular aspects from each of the devices and putting them together into a larger puzzle.

Sensor fusion is a tough task. There are some devices that might not be working at the time of the sensor capture. Or, there might some devices that are unable to report well what they have detected. Again, using a human analogy, suppose you are in a dark room and so your eyes cannot see much. At that point, you might need to rely more so on your ears and what you hear. The same is true for a self-driving car. If the cameras are obscured due to snow and sleet, it might be that the radar can provide a greater indication of what the external conditions consist of.

In the case of a self-driving car, there can be a plethora of such sensory devices. Each is reporting what it can. Each might have its difficulties. Each might have its limitations, such as how far ahead it can detect an object. All of these limitations need to be considered during the sensor fusion task.

D-03: Virtual World Model

For humans, we presumably keep in our minds a model of the world around us when we are driving a car. In your mind, you know that the car is going at say 60 miles per hour and that you are on a freeway. You have a model in your mind that your car is surrounded by other cars, and that there are lanes to the freeway. Your model is not only based on what you can see, hear, etc., but also what you know about the nature of the world. You know that at any moment that car ahead of you can smash on its brakes, or the car behind you can ram into your car, or that the truck in the next lane might swerve into your lane.

The AI of the self-driving car needs to have a virtual world model, which it then keeps updated with whatever it is receiving from the sensor fusion, which received its input from the sensor capture and the sensory devices.

D-04: System Action Plan

By having a virtual world model, the AI of the self-driving car is able to keep track of where the car is and what is happening around the car. In addition, the AI needs to determine what to do next. Should the self-driving car hit its brakes? Should the self-driving car stay in its lane or swerve into the lane to the left? Should the self-driving car accelerate or slow down?

A system action plan needs to be prepared by the AI of the self-driving car. The action plan specifies what actions should be taken. The actions need to pertain to the status of the virtual world model. Plus, the actions need to be realizable.

This realizability means that the AI cannot just assert that the self-driving car should suddenly sprout wings and fly. Instead, the AI must be bound by whatever the self-driving car can actually do, such as coming to a halt in a distance of X feet at a speed of Y miles per hour, rather than perhaps asserting that the self-driving car come to a halt in 0 feet as though it could instantaneously come to a stop while it is in motion.

D-05: Controls Activation

The system action plan is implemented by activating the controls of the car to act according to what the plan stipulates. This might mean that the accelerator control is commanded to increase the speed of the car. Or, the steering control is commanded to turn the steering wheel 30 degrees to the left or right.

One question arises as to whether or not the controls respond as they are commanded to do. In other words, suppose the AI has commanded the accelerator to increase, but for some reason it does not do so. Or, maybe it tries to do so, but the speed of the car does not increase. The controls activation feeds back into the virtual world model, and simultaneously the virtual world model is getting updated from the sensors, the sensor capture, and the sensor fusion. This allows the AI to ascertain what has taken place as a result of the controls being commanded to take some kind of action.

By the way, please keep in mind that though the diagram seems to have a linear progression to it, the reality is that these are all aspects of the self-driving car that are happening in parallel and simultaneously. The sensors are capturing data, meanwhile the sensor fusion is taking place, meanwhile the virtual model is being updated, meanwhile the system action plan is being formulated and reformulated, meanwhile the controls are being activated.

This is the same as a human being that is driving a car. They are eyeballing the road, meanwhile they are fusing in their mind the sights, sounds, etc., meanwhile their mind is updating their model of the world around them, meanwhile they are formulating an action plan of what to do, and meanwhile they are pushing their foot onto the pedals and steering the car. In the normal course of driving a car, you are doing all of these at once. I mention this so that when you look at the diagram, you will think of the boxes as processes that are all happening at the same time, and not as though only one happens and then the next.

They are shown diagrammatically in a simplistic manner to help comprehend what is taking place. You though should also realize that they are working in parallel and simultaneous with each other. This is a tough aspect in that the inter-element communications involve latency and other aspects that must be taken into account. There can be delays in one element updating and then sharing its latest status with other elements.

D-06: Automobile & CAN

Contemporary cars use various automotive electronics and a Controller Area Network (CAN) to serve as the components that underlie the driving aspects of a car. There are Electronic Control Units (ECU's) which control subsystems of the car, such as the engine, the brakes, the doors, the windows, and so on.

The elements D-01, D-02, D-03, D-04, D-05 are layered on top of the D-06, and must be aware of the nature of what the D-06 is able to do and not do.

D-07: In-Car Commands

Humans are going to be occupants in self-driving cars. In a Level 5 self-driving car, there must be some form of communication that takes place between the humans and the self-driving car. For example, I go into a self-driving car and tell it that I want to be driven over to Disneyland, and along the way I want to stop at In-and-Out Burger. The self-driving car now parses what I've said and tries to then establish a means to carry out my wishes.

In-car commands can happen at any time during a driving journey. Though my example was about an in-car command when I first got into my self-driving car, it could be that while the self-driving car is carrying out the journey that I change my mind. Perhaps after getting stuck in traffic, I tell the self-driving car to forget about getting the burgers and just head straight over to the theme park. The self-driving car needs to be alert to in-car commands throughout the journey.

D-08: VX2 Communications

We will ultimately have self-driving cars communicating with each other, doing so via V2V (Vehicle-to-Vehicle) communications. We will also have self-driving cars that communicate with the roadways and other aspects of the transportation infrastructure, doing so via V2I (Vehicle-to-Infrastructure).

The variety of ways in which a self-driving car will be communicating with other cars and infrastructure is being called V2X, whereby the letter X means whatever else we identify as something that a car should or would want to communicate with. The V2X communications will be taking place simultaneous with everything else on the diagram, and those other elements will need to incorporate whatever it gleans from those V2X communications.

D-09: Deep Learning

The use of Deep Learning permeates all other aspects of the self-driving car. The AI of the self-driving car will be using deep learning to do a better job at the systems action plan, and at the controls activation, and at the sensor fusion, and so on.

Currently, the use of artificial neural networks is the most prevalent form of deep learning. Based on large swaths of data, the neural networks attempt to "learn" from the data and therefore direct the efforts of the self-driving car accordingly.

D-10: Tactical AI

Tactical AI is the element of dealing with the moment-to-moment driving of the self-driving car. Is the self-driving car staying in its lane of the freeway? Is the car responding appropriately to the controls commands? Are the sensory devices working?

For human drivers, the tactical equivalent can be seen when you watch a novice driver such as a teenager that is first driving. They are focused on the mechanics of the driving task, keeping their eye on the road while also trying to properly control the car.

D-11: Strategic AI

The Strategic AI aspects of a self-driving car are dealing with the larger picture of what the self-driving car is trying to do. If I had asked that the self-driving car take me to Disneyland, there is an overall journey map that needs to be kept and maintained.

There is an interaction between the Strategic AI and the Tactical AI. The Strategic AI is wanting to keep on the mission of the driving, while the Tactical AI is focused on the particulars underway in the driving effort. If the Tactical AI seems to wander away from the overarching mission, the Strategic AI wants to see why and get things back on track. If the Tactical AI realizes that there is something amiss on the self-driving car, it needs to alert the Strategic AI accordingly and have an adjustment to the overarching mission that is underway.

D-12: Self-Aware AI

Very few of the self-driving cars being developed are including a Self-Aware AI element, which we at the Cybernetic Self-Driving Car Institute believe is crucial to Level 5 self-driving cars.

The Self-Aware AI element is intended to watch over itself, in the sense that the AI is making sure that the AI is working as intended. Suppose you had a human driving a car, and they were starting to drive erratically. Hopefully, their own self-awareness would make them realize they themselves are driving poorly, such as perhaps starting to fall asleep after having been driving for hours on end. If you had a passenger in the car, they might be able to alert the driver if the driver is starting to do something amiss. This is exactly what the Self-Aware

AI element tries to do, it becomes the overseer of the AI, and tries to detect when the AI has become faulty or confused, and then find ways to overcome the issue.

D-13: Economic

The economic aspects of a self-driving car are not per se a technology aspect of a self-driving car, but the economics do indeed impact the nature of a self-driving car. For example, the cost of outfitting a self-driving car with every kind of possible sensory device is prohibitive, and so choices need to be made about which devices are used. And, for those sensory devices chosen, whether they would have a full set of features or a more limited set of features.

We are going to have self-driving cars that are at the low-end of a consumer cost point, and others at the high-end of a consumer cost point. You cannot expect that the self-driving car at the low-end is going to be as robust as the one at the high-end. I realize that many of the self-driving car pundits are acting as though all self-driving cars will be the same, but they won't be. Just like anything else, we are going to have self-driving cars that have a range of capabilities. Some will be better than others. Some will be safer than others. This is the way of the real-world, and so we need to be thinking about the economics aspects when considering the nature of self-driving cars.

D-14: Societal

This component encompasses the societal aspects of AI which also impacts the technology of self-driving cars. For example, the famous Trolley Problem involves what choices should a self-driving car make when faced with life-and-death matters. If the self-driving car is about to either hit a child standing in the roadway, or instead ram into a tree at the side of the road and possibly kill the humans in the self-driving car, which choice should be made?

We need to keep in mind the societal aspects will underlie the AI of the self-driving car. Whether we are aware of it explicitly or not, the AI will have embedded into it various societal assumptions.

D-15: Innovation

I included the notion of innovation into the framework because we can anticipate that whatever a self-driving car consists of, it will continue to be innovated over time. The self-driving cars coming out in the next several years will undoubtedly be different and less innovative than the versions that come out in ten years hence, and so on.

Framework Overall

For those of you that want to learn about self-driving cars, you can potentially pick a particular element and become specialized in that aspect. Some engineers are focusing on the sensory devices. Some engineers focus on the controls activation. And so on. There are specialties in each of the elements.

Researchers are likewise specializing in various aspects. For example, there are researchers that are using Deep Learning to see how best it can be used for sensor fusion. There are other researchers that are using Deep Learning to derive good System Action Plans. Some are studying how to develop AI for the Strategic aspects of the driving task, while others are focused on the Tactical aspects.

A well-prepared all-around software developer that is involved in self-driving cars should be familiar with all of the elements, at least to the degree that they know what each element does. This is important since whatever piece of the pie that the software developer works on, they need to be knowledgeable about what the other elements are doing.

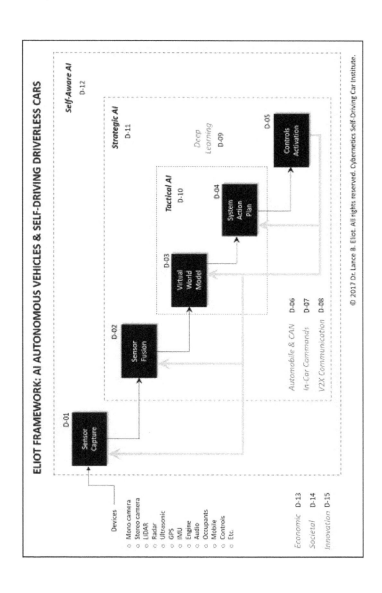

ELIOT FRAMEWORK: AI AUTONOMOUS VEHICLES & SELF-DRIVING DRIVERLESS CARS

CHAPTER 2

API'S AND SELF-DRIVING CARS

CHAPTER 2
API'S AND
SELF-DRIVING CARS

API's have become the darling of the high-tech software world. There are conferences devoted to the topic of API's. Non-tech business-oriented magazines and journals gush about the importance of API's. Anyone that makes a software package nowadays is nearly forced into providing API's.

It's the rise of the Application Programming Interface (API).

Rather than being something magical, it's actually just the providing of a portal into a software system that otherwise might be difficult to communicate with. One major advantage of a portal is that it can allow various extensions that can add-on to the software system and go beyond what the original software system itself can accomplish. You can also interface to the original software system and allow it to become interconnected with other software. And, you can avoid potentially having to redevelop the wheel, so to speak, by leveraging whatever capabilities the original software system has. Some would say it also allows the software to be at a higher level of abstraction.

I've written extensively about API's for AI systems, which you can read about in Chapter 3 and Chapter 4 of my book "AI Guardian Angel Bots for Deep AI Trustworthiness: Practical Advances in Artificial Intelligence (AI) and Machine Learning" (available on Amazon).

By providing a healthy set of API's, the developers of the original software system are able to encourage the emergence of a third-party add-on ecosystem. This in turn will help make the original software system more popular as others connect to it and rely upon it. Eventually, with some luck and skill, the original software system becomes immersed in so many other areas of life that it becomes undeniably necessary. What might have begun as a small effort can snowball into a widespread and highly known cornerstone for an entire marketplace radiating outward from the original software core.

With great promise often comes great peril. In the case of API's, there is a chance that the use of the API's can boomerang on a company that made the original software system. These portals can be used as intended and yet cause undesirable results, along with them being used for unintended nefarious reasons and also causing undesirable results.

Let's consider the case of an API used as intended, but has caused what some perceive as an undesirable result. This particular example involving Gmail has been in the news recently and led to some untoward attention and concerns.

Google allows for API's to connect to Gmail. This would seem to be handy since it would allow other software developers to connect their software with Gmail. This can provide handy new capabilities for Gmail that otherwise would have never existed. Meanwhile, those software developers that might have written something that would have never seen the light of day, might be able to piggyback onto the popularity of Gmail and hit themselves a homerun.

When an app that is able to connect to Gmail via the API is first run, it usually asks the user whether they are OK with the app connecting into their Gmail. For many users, they often don't read the fine print on these kinds of messages and are so eager to get the app that they just say yes to anything that the app displays when being installed. Or, the user might be tempted to read what the conditions are, but it is so lengthy and written in arcane legalese that they don't do so, and often wonder whether they maybe have given up their first born child by agreeing to the app's conditions. It's a combination of the app at times being tricky about explaining what's up, and the end-user not diligently making sure that they know what they signing up for.

Typically, once the user agrees to the app request at first install, Google then grants to the app that it can access the Gmail of that user. This includes being able to access their emails. The app can potentially read the contents of those emails. It can potentially delete emails. It can potentially send emails on behalf of the user.

In recent widespread news reports, the media caused a stir by finding some companies that read the user's Gmail emails via AI, doing so to try and figure out what interests the person has and possibly then hit them with ads. In some cases, the emails are even read by humans at the software company, presumably for purposes of being able to gauge how well the AI is doing the reading of the emails. There are also some firms that provide the emails or snapshots of the emails to other third-parties that they have deals with. All in all, it was a bit of a shock to many people that they had provided such access to their "private" email.

I realize that many software developers would blame the user on this – how dumb can you be to go ahead and agree to have your emails accessed and then later on complain that it is taking place? As I mentioned earlier, many users aren't aware they are doing so, or might be vaguely aware but not really put together two-plus-two and fully understand the implications of what they have allowed to happen. There are some software developers that insist their app is doing a service for the user, and by reading their emails it is helping to target them with things that the person is interested in. That's a bit of a stretch and for many users the logic doesn't ring true to them.

You might remember the case of McDonald's in India and the API that allowed personal information of the McDelivery mobile app to be leaked out. The API connection, normally intended for useful and proper uses, also allowed access to the name, phone numbers, home address, email addresses, and other private info. This was unintended and was an undesirable result.

Hackers Love API's

As you might guess, hackers love it when there are API's. It gives them hope that there might be a means to sneakily "break into" a system. I've likened this to a fortress that has all sorts of fortified locked doors, which also provides a window that someone with a bit of extra effort can use to get into the fort. Software companies often spend a tremendous amount of effort to try and make their software impervious to security breaches and attacks, and yet then provide an API that exposes aspects that undermine all the rest of their security.

How could that happen? Wouldn't the API's get as much scrutiny as the rest of the system in terms of becoming secure? The answer is that no, the API's often don't get as much scrutiny. The perception of the company making the software is that the API's are some kind of techie detail and there's no need to make sure those are tight. In my experience, most software firms happily provide the API's in hopes that someone will want to use them, and aren't nearly as concerned that those that might use them would do so for nefarious reasons.

The API's are often classified into these three groupings:
- Private
- Partner
- Public

API's that are considered private are usually intended to be used solely by the firm making the software. They setup the API's for their own convenience. This also though often means that the API's have a lot of power and can access all sorts of aspects of the software. The firm figures that's Okay since only the firm itself will presumably be using the API's. These are often either undocumented and just known amongst those that developed the software, or there is written documentation but it is kept inside the firm and written for those that are insiders.

API's that are oriented toward partners are intended to be used by allied firms that the firm making the software decides to cut some kind of deal with. Maybe I make a software package that does sales and marketing kinds of functions, while a firm I cut a deal with has a software package for accounting and wants to connect with my package. Once again, the assumption is that only authorized developers with firms that are properly engaged with will use these API's. The power of the access by these API's is once again relatively high, but usually less than the private API's since the original developers often don't want the third-party to mess-up and do great harm. The documentation often is a bit more elaborated than the private API's since the partner firm and its developers need to know what the API's do.

API's of a public nature are intended to be used by anyone that wants to access the software. These are often very limited in their access capabilities and are considered potential threats to the system. Thus, only the need-to-know aspects are usually made available. The documentation can sometimes be very elaborate and extensive, while in other cases the documentation is slim and the assumption is that people will figure it out on their own or they might share amongst each other as they figure out what the API's do.

What sometimes happens is that a firm provides say public API's, and secretly has partner API's and private API's. Those developers that opt to use the public API's become curious about the partner API's, and either figure them out on their own, or convince a partner to leak details about what they are. If the partner API's can be used, the next step is to go after the private API's. It can become a stepwise progression to figuring out the whole set of API's.

The API's are often classified into whether they do this:
- Perform an action
- Provide object access

Let's consider first the performing an action type of API. This allows an app invoking the API to request that the original software perform an action that has been made available via the API. For example, suppose there's a car that has an electronic on-board system and there's an API associated with the system. You develop a mobile app that connects to the on-board electronic system and you opt to use the API to invoke an action that the electronic system is capable of performing. Suppose the action consists of honking the horn. Your mobile app then connects to the on-board electronic system and via the API requests the electronic system to honk the horn, which it then dutifully does. Honk, honk.

Or, an app might seek to get access to an object and do so via the API. Suppose the electronic on-board system of the car has data in it that includes the name of the car owner and vehicle info such as the make, model, and number of miles driven. The developers of the electronic on-board system might make available an API that allows for access to the "car owner object" that has that data. You then create an app that connects to the electronic on-board car system and asks via the API to access the car owner object. Once the object is provided, your app then reads the data and now can display it on the screen of the mobile app.

How does this apply to AI self-driving cars?

At the Cybernetic AI Self-Driving Car Institute, we are developing AI software for self-driving cars. This includes providing API's, and also involves making use of API's provided by other allied software systems and components.

If you've ever played with the API for the Tesla, you likely know that you can get access to vehicle information, vehicle settings, and the like. You can also invoke actions such as honking the horn, waking up the car, starting the charging of the car, setting the car climate controls, open the trunk, and so on. It's fun and exciting to create your own mobile app to do these things. That being said, there is already a mobile app provided by Tesla that does these things, so it really doesn't payoff to create them yourself, other than the personal satisfaction involved and also to explore the nature of API's on cars, or if you are trying to develop your own third-party app and want to avoid or circumvent the official one.

One of the crucial aspects about API's for cars is that a car is a life-or-death matter. It's one thing to provide API's to an on-board entertainment center, allowing you to write an app that can connect to it and play your favorite songs. Not much of a life or death matter there. On the other hand, if the car provides API's that allow for actual car controls aspects, it could be something much more dangerous and of concern.

Now that I've dragged you through the fundamentals of API's, it gets us to some important points:

- What kind of API's, if any, should an AI self-driving car provide?
- If the API's are provided for an AI self-driving car, how will they be protected from misuse?
- If the API's are provided for an AI self-driving car, how will they be tested to ensure their veracity?
- Etc.

Some auto makers and tech firms are indicating they will not provide any API's regarding their AI self-driving cars. That's their prerogative and we'll have to see if that's a good strategy.

Some are making private API's and trying to be secretive about it. The question always arises, how can you keep it secret and what happens if the secret gets discovered.

Some are making partner API's and letting their various business partners know about it. This can be handy, though as mentioned earlier it might start other third-parties down the path of figuring out the partner API's and then next aiming at the private API's.

Overall, it's a mixed bag as to the various AI self-driving car firms are opting to deal with API's.

There's also another twist to the API topic for AI self-driving cars, namely:

- API's for Self-Driving Car On-Board System
  - API for the AI portion
  - API for non-AI portions

- API's for Self-Driving Car Cloud-based System
  - API for the AI portion
  - API for non-AI portions

There can be API's for the on-board systems of the self-driving car, and there can be other API's for the cloud-based system of the self-driving car. Most AI self-driving cars are going to have OTA (Over The Air) capabilities to interact with a cloud-based system established by the auto maker or tech firm. From a third-party perspective, it would be handy to be able to communicate with the software that's in the cloud over OTA, in addition to the software that's on-board the self-driving car.

Some AI developers think it is crazy talk to allow API's for the self-driving car on-board systems. They believe that the on-board systems are sacrosanct and that nobody but nobody should be poking around in them. Likewise, there are AI developers that believe fervently that there should not be API's allowed for the cloud-based systems associated with self-driving cars. They perceive that this could lead to incredible troubles, since it might somehow allow someone to do something untoward that could then get spread to all of the self-driving cars that connect to the cloud-based system.

There are some auto makers and tech firms that want to provide API's, which they do so in hopes that their AI self-driving car will become more popular than their competition. As mentioned earlier, if you can get a thriving third-party ecosystem going, it can greatly help boost your core system and get it to become more enmeshed into the marketplace. Also, if you have only one hundred developers in your company, they can only do so much, but if you can have thousands upon thousands of "developers" that write more software to connect to your system, you have magnified greatly your programming reach.

Innocent API's Promise Not to Endanger

It is believed by some that the API's can be provided for aspects that don't endanger the self-driving car and its occupants, these are so-called innocent API's.

Suppose for example that the API's only allow for retrieval of information from the AI and the self-driving car. This presumably would prevent someone from getting the AI self-driving car to perform an undue action. Just make available API's for object access, but none that allow for performing an action. You can still criticize this and suggest there might be a privacy of information loss due to object access the API's, but at least it isn't going to directly commandeer the AI self-driving car.

Another viewpoint is that it is Okay to allow for action performing API's, but those API's would be constrained to only narrow and presumably safe actions. Suppose you have an API that allows for honking the horn or for flashing the lights of the car? Those seem innocuous. That being said, I suppose if you honk the horn at the wrong time it can confuse pedestrians and maybe also scare people. Similarly, flashing the lights of the car at the wrong time might be alarming to another human driver of a human driven car. Generally, those don't seem overly unsafe per se.

There are five core stages of an AI self-driving car while in action:
- Sensors data collection and interpretation
- Sensor fusion
- Virtual world model updating
- AI action planning
- Car controls commands issuance

If there was an API for the retrieval of information from the sensors data collection and interpretation, this would seem to be innocuous. Indeed, it might allow a clever third-party to develop add-on's that could do some impressive augmentation to the sensor analysis. You could potentially also grab the data and push it through other machine learning models to try and find better ways to interpret the data. As mentioned before, this could though have privacy and other complications.

For the sensor fusion, suppose you provided an API that would allow for invoking of some subroutines that combine together the radar data and the LIDAR data. This raises all sorts of potential issues. Will this undermine the validity of the system? Will this consume on-board computer resources and possibly starve other mission critical elements? And so on.

The same concerns can be raised about API's that might invoke actions of the virtual world model, or actions involving the AI action plan updating. The same is the case for toying with the car controls commands issuance. Indeed, any kind of taxing of those components, even if only for data retrieval, would have to be done in such a manner that it does not simultaneously slow down or distract those aspects while they are working.

We must also consider that there can be a difference between what an API was intended to do, and what it actually does. If the auto maker or tech firm was not careful, they could have provided an API that is only supposed to honk the horn, but that if used in some other manner it can suddenly (let's pretend) change the steering direction of the self-driving car. This shouldn't happen, of course, and could produce deadly consequences. It wasn't intended to happen. But inadvertently, while creating the API, the developers made a hole that allowed for this to occur. Some determined hackers might discover that the API has this other purpose.

Now, I am sure that some of you will say that even if there is something untoward in an API capability, all the auto maker or tech firm needs to do is send out an update via the OTA and close off that back-door. Yes, kind of. First, the auto maker or tech firm has to even find out that the back-door exists. Then, they need to create the plug or fix, and test it to make sure it doesn't produce some other untoward result. They then need to push it out to the self-driving cars via the

OTA. The self-driving cars have to have their OTA enabled and download the plug or fix, and install it. All of this can take time, and meanwhile the self-driving cars are "exposed" in terms of someone taking a nefarious advantage of the hole.

The API's are often setup with authentication that requires any connecting system to have proper authority to access the API. This is a handy and important security feature. That being said, it is not necessarily an impenetrable barrier to still use the API. Remember the story of the app that gains access to your Gmail when you first install the app by getting your permission to do so. Suppose you are installing an app on your smartphone, which you've already connected to your AI self-driving car, and you are asked by the app to allow it to access the API's in your self-driving car. You indicate yes, not knowing that ramifications this could have.

Will AI self-driving car makers provide API's? Will they provide SDK's (Software Development Kits)? Will they discourage or encourage so-called "hot wiring" of AI self-driving cars? Perhaps the path will be to limit any such capabilities to only on-board entertainment systems and not at all to any kind of car control or driving task elements.

Without such API's, presumably the AI self-driving car might be safer, but will it also lose out on the possible bonanza of all sorts of third-party add-ons that will make your AI self-driving car superior to others and become the defacto standard AI self-driving car that everyone wants. We'll have to wait and see how the API wars plays out.

CHAPTER 3

EGOCENTRIC DESIGNS AND SELF-DRIVING CARS

CHAPTER 3

EGOCENTRIC DESIGNS AND SELF-DRIVING CARS

You might find of interest the social psychology aspect known as the actor-observer effect. Before I explain what it is, allow me to provide you with a small story of something that happened the other day.

I was chatting with an AI developer that is creating software for an auto maker and he had approached me after I had finished talking at an industry conference. During my speech, I had mentioned several so-called "edge" cases involving AI self-driving cars. These edge cases involved aspects such as an AI self-driving car being able to navigate safely and properly a roundabout or traffic circle, and being able to navigate safely an accident scene, and so on.

At the Cybernetic AI Self-Driving Car Institute, we are developing AI software for self-driving cars and also advising other firms about the matter too. Thus, we're working on quite a number of edge problems.

Well, the AI developer was curious why I cared about the "edge" problems in AI self-driving cars.

An edge problem is one that is not considered at the core of a system. It is considered less vital and an aspect that you can presumably come around and solve at a later time, after you've finished up the core.

This is not a hard-and-fast rule in the sense that something that one person thinks is an edge might truly be part of the core. Or, something that is an edge might not be at the core but that otherwise without the edge you are going to have a very limited and potentially brittle core.

Edges are often in the eyes of the beholder. Thus, be careful when someone tosses out there that some feature or capability or issue is an "edge" problem. It's an easy means to deflect attention and distract you from realizing that maybe the edge is truly needed, or that the core you are going to be getting will fall apart because it fails to solve an edge aspect. I've seen many people be dismissive of something important by trying to label it as an edge problem. This is a sneaky way at times to avoid having to cover an aspect, and instead pretend that it is inconsequential. Oh, that's just an edge, someone will assert, and then walk away from the conversation or drop the microphone, as it were.

Anyway, back to my chat with the AI developer. I asked him why he was curious that I was so serious about the various edge problems of AI self-driving cars. It seemed relatively self-evident that these are aspects that can occur in real-world driving situations and that if we are going to have AI self-driving cars that are on our roadways we ought to be able to expect that those self-driving cars can handle everyday driving circumstances. Self-driving cars are a life-and-death matter. If an AI self-driving car cannot handle the driving tasks at-hand, things can get mighty dangerous.

His reply was that there was no particular need to deal with these various "edge" problems. As an example, I asked him what would his AI do when it encountered a driving situation involving a roundabout or traffic circle (I'm sure you know what these are — they are areas where cars go around a circle to then get to an exit radiating from the circle)?

He replied that it wouldn't have to deal with it. The GPS would have alerted his AI that a roundabout was upcoming, and his AI would simply route itself another way. By avoiding the "edge" problem, he said that it no longer mattered.

Really, I asked?

I pointed out that suppose the GPS did not have it marked and thus the self-driving car went into the roundabout anyway? Or, suppose the GPS wasn't working properly and so the AI self-driving car blindly went to the roundabout. Even if the GPS did indicate it was there, suppose that there was no viable alternative route and that the self-driving car would have to proceed through the roundabout? Was it supposed to always take the long way, assuming that such a path was even available? This reminded me of a teenage driver that I knew that avoided roundabouts because he was scared of them.

He insisted that none of these aspects would occur. He stood steadfast that there was no need to worry about it. He said I might as well say that suppose aliens from Mars came down to earth. Should he need to have his AI cope with that too?

The Pogo Stick Problem

This brings up another example that's been making the hallways of AI developers for auto makers and tech firms doing self-driving cars systems. It's the pogo stick problem. The AI self-driving car is going down a street, minding its own business (so to speak), and all of a sudden a human on a pogo stick bounces into the road and directly in front of the self-driving car. What does the AI do?

One answer that some have asserted is that this will never happen. They retort that the odds of a person being on a pogo stick is extremely remote. If there was such a circumstance, the odds that the person on the pogo stick would go out into the street is even further remote. And, the odds that they would do this just as a car was approaching was even more so remote, since why would someone be stupid enough to pogo stick into traffic and endanger getting hit?

In this viewpoint, we are at some kind of odds that are like getting hit by lightning. In fact, they would say it's even lesser odds and more like getting hit by lightning twice in a row.

I am not so sure that the probability of this happening is quite as low as they would claim. They are also suggesting or implying that the probability is zero. This seems like a false suggestion since I think we can all agree there is a chance it could happen. No matter how small a chance, it is definitely more than zero.

Those that buy into the zero probability belief will then refuse to discuss the matter any further. They say it is like discussing the tooth fairy, so why waste time on something that will never happen. There are some that I can at least get them to consider that suppose it did happen, even if really remote odds. What then?

They then seem to divide into one of two camps. There's the camp that says if the human was stupid enough to pogo stick into the road and directly in front of the self-driving car, whatever happens next is their fault. If the AI detects them and screeches the car to a halt and still hits them, because there wasn't enough distance between them and the self-driving car, that's the fault of the stupid human on the pogo stick. Case closed.

The other camp says that we shouldn't allow humans on pogo sticks to go out onto the road. They believe that the matter should be a legal one, outlawing people from using pogo sticks on streets. When I point out that even if there was such a law, it is conceivable that a "law breaker" (like say a child on the pogo stick, which I guess might be facing a life of crime by using it in the streets), might wander unknowingly into the street. What then? The reply to that is that we need to put up barriers to prevent pogo stick riding humans from going out into the streets. All I can say is imagine a world in which we have tall barriers on all streets across all of the United States so that we won't have pogo stick wandering kids. Imagine that!

If you think these kinds of arguments seem somewhat foolish in that why not just make the AI of the self-driving car so it can deal with a pogo stick riding human, you are perhaps starting to see what I call egocentric design of AI self-driving cars.

There are some firms and some AI developers that look at the world through the eyes of the self-driving car. What's best for the self-driving car is the way that the world should be, in their view. If pogo riding humans are a pest for self-driving cars, get rid of the pests, so to speak, by outlawing those humans or do something like erecting a barrier to keep them from becoming a problem. Why should the AI need to shoulder the hassle of those pogo stick riding humans? Solve the problem by instead controlling the environment.

For those of you that are standing outside of this kind of viewpoint, you likely find it to be somewhat a bizarre perspective. It likely seems to you that it is real-world impractical to consider controlling the environment. The environment is what it is. Take it as a given. Make your darned AI good enough to deal with it. Expect that humans on pogo sticks are going to happen. Live with it.

What's even more damming is that there are lots of variants beyond just a pogo stick riding human that could fall into the same classification of sorts. Suppose a human on a scooter suddenly went into the street in front of the self-driving car? Isn't that the same class of problem? And, isn't it pretty good odds that with the recent advent of ridesharing scooters that we'll see this happening more and more?

If you are perplexed that anybody of their right mind could somehow believe that the AI of a self-driving car does not need to deal with the pogo stick riding human, and worse still the scooter riding human that is more likely prevalent, you might be interested in the actor-observer effect.

Here's the background about the actor-observer effect.

Suppose we put someone into a room to do some work, let's make it office type of work. We'll have a one-way mirror that allows you to stand outside the room and watch what the person is doing. Let's pretend that the person in the room is unaware that they are being observed. We'll refer to the person in the room as an "actor" and we'll refer to you standing outside the room as the "observer."

At first, there will be work brought into the room, some kind of paperwork to be done, and it will be given to the actor. They are supposed to work on this paperwork task. You are watching them and so far all seems relatively normal and benign. They do the work. You can see that they are doing the work. The work is getting accomplished.

Next, the amount of work brought into the room starts to increase. The actor begins to sweat as they are genuinely trying to keep up with the volume of paperwork to be processed. Even more paperwork is brought into the room. Now the actor starts to get frantic. It's way too much work. It is beginning to pile up. The actor is getting strained and you can see that they are obviously unable to get the work completed.

We stop the experiment.

If we were to ask you what happened, as an observer you would likely say that the person doing the work was incapable to keep up with the work required. The actor was low performing. Had the actor done a better job, they presumably could have kept up. They didn't seem to know or find a means to be efficient enough to get the work done.

If we were to ask the actor what happened, they would likely say that they were doing good at the start, but then the environment went wacky. They were inundated with an unfair amount of paperwork. Nobody could have coped with it. They did the best they could do.
Which of these is right – the actor or the observer?

Perspective Determines What is Seen

It's not so much about right or wrong, as it is the perspective of the matter. Usually, an actor or the person in the middle or midst of an activity tends to look at themselves as the stable part and the environment as the uncontrollable part. Meanwhile, the observer tends to see the environment as the part that is given, and it is the actor that becomes the focus of attention.

If you are a manager, you might have encountered this same kind of phenomena when you first started managing other people. You have someone working for you that seems to not be keeping up. They argue that it is because they are being given an unfair amount of work to do. You meanwhile believe they are being given a fair amount of work and it is their performance that's at fault. You, and the person you are managing, can end-up endlessly going round and round about this, caught in a nearly hopeless deadlock. Each of you likely becoming increasingly insistent that the other one is not seeing things the right way.

It is likely due to the actor-observer effect, namely:

- When you are in an observer position, you tend to see the environment as a given. The thing that needs to change is the actor.

- When you are in the actor position, you tend to see the environment as something that needs to be changed, and you are the given.

Until both parties realize the impact of this effect, it becomes very hard to carry on a balanced discussion. Otherwise, it's like looking at a painting that one of you insists is red, and the other insists is blue. Neither of you will be able to discuss the painting in other more useful terms until you realize that you each are seeing a particular color that maybe makes sense depending upon the nature of your eyes and your cornea.

Let's then revisit the AI developer that I spoke with at the conference. Recall that he was insistent that the edge problems were not important. For the pogo stick riding human example, the "problem" at hand was the stupid human. I was saying that the problem was that the AI was insufficient to cope with the pogo stick riding human. Why did we not see eye to eye?

His focus was on the self-driving car. In a sense, he's like the actor in the actor-observer effect. His view was that the environment was the problem and so all you need to do is change the wacky environment. My view was that of the "observer" in that I assert the environment is a given, and you need to make the "actor" up to snuff to deal with that environment.

This then brings us to the egocentric design of AI self-driving cars. There are many auto makers and tech firms that are filled with AI developers and teams that view the world from the perspective of the AI self-driving car. They want the world to fit to what their AI self-driving car can do. This could be considered "egocentric" because it elevates the AI of the self-driving car in terms of being the focus. It does what it does. What it can't do, that's tough for the rest of us. Live with it.

For the rest of us, we tend to say wait a second, they need to make the AI self-driving car do whatever the environment requires. Putting an AI self-driving car onto our roadways is something that is a privilege and they need to consider it as such. It is on the shoulders of the AI developers and the auto makers and tech firms to make that AI self-driving car deal with whatever comes its way.

Believe it or not, I've had some of these auto makers and tech firms that have said we ought to have special roads just for AI self-driving cars. The reason for this is that whenever I point out that self-driving cars will need to mix with human driven cars, and so the AI needs to know how to deal with cars around it that are being driven by "unpredictable" humans, the answer I get is that we should devote special roads for AI self-driving cars. Divide the AI self-driving cars from those pesky human drivers.

There are some AI developers that dream wishfully of the day that there are only AI self-driving cars on our roadways. I point out that's not going to happen for a very long time. In the United States alone we have 200 million conventional cars. Those are not going away overnight. If we are going to be introducing true Level 5 self-driving cars onto our roadways, it is going to be done in a mixture with human driven cars. As such, the AI has to assume there will be human driven cars and needs to be able to cope with those human driven cars.

The solution voiced by some AI developers is to separate the AI self-driving cars from the human driven cars. For example, convert the HOV lanes into AI self-driving car only lanes. I then ask them what happens when a human driven car decides to swerve into the HOV lane that has AI self-driving cars? Their answer is that the HOV lanes need to have barriers to prevent this from happening. And so on, with the reply always dealing with changing the environment to make this feasible. What about motorcycles? Answer, make sure the barriers will prevent motorcycles from going into the HOV lane. What about animals that wander onto the highway? Answer, the barriers should prevent animals or put up other additional barriers on the sides of the highway to prevent animals from wandering in.

After seeing how far they'll go on this, I eventually get them to a point that I ask if maybe we ought to consider the AI self-driving car to be similar to a train. Right now, we usually cordon off train tracks. We put barriers to prevent anything from wandering into the path of the train. We put up signs warning about the train is coming. Isn't that what they are arguing for? Namely, AI self-driving cars are to be treated like trains?

But, if that's the case, I don't quite then see where the AI part of the self-driving cars enters into things. Why not just make some kind of simpleton software that treats each car like it is part of a train. You then have these semi-automated cars that come together and collect into a series of cars like a train does. They then proceed along as a train. There are some that have even proposed this, though I'll grant them that at least they view this as something like a "smart" colony of self-driving cars that come together when needed, but then still are individual "intelligent" self-driving once they leave the hive.

Those that are making AI self-driving cars need to look past an egocentric view. We are not going to have true AI self-driving cars if we continue to try and limit the environment. A true level 5 self-driving car is supposed to be able to drive a car like a human would. If that's the case, we then ought to not have to change anything per se about the existing driving environment. If humans can drive it, the AI should be able to do the same. I tried to explain this to the AI developer. I'm not sure that my words made much sense, since I think he was still seeing the painting as entirely in the color of red, while I was talking about the color blue. Maybe my words herein about the actor-observer effect might aid him in seeing the situation from both sides. I certainly hope so.

CHAPTER 4
FAMILY ROAD TRIPS
AND
SELF-DRIVING CARS

CHAPTER 4

FAMILY ROAD TRIPS
AND
SELF-DRIVING CARS

Have you ever taken a road trip across the United States with your family? It's considered a core part of Americana to make such a trip. Somewhat immortalized by the now classic movie National Lampoon's Vacation, the film showcased the doting scatter brained father Clark Griswold with his caring wife, Ellen, and their vacation-with-your-parents trapped children, Rusty and Audrey, as they all at times either enjoyed or managed to endure a cross-country expedition of a life time.

As is typically portrayed in such situations, the father drives the car for most of the trip and serves as the taskmaster to keep the trip moving forward, the mother provides soothing care for the family and tries to keep things on an even keel, and the children must contend with parents that are out-of-touch with reality and that are jointly determined that come heck-or-high-water their kids will presumably have a good time (at least by the definition of the parents). The move was released in 1983 and became a blockbuster that spawned other variants. Today, we can find fault with how the nuclear family is portrayed and the stereotypes used throughout the movie, but nonetheless it put on film what generally is known as the family road trip.

What does this have to do with AI self-driving cars?

At the Cybernetic AI Self-Driving Car Institute, we are developing AI systems for self-driving cars and doing so with an eye towards how people will want to use AI self-driving cars. It is important to consider the behavior of how human occupants will be while inside an AI self-driving car and therefore astutely design and build AI self-driving cars accordingly.

In a conventional car, for a family road trip, it is pretty much the case that the parents sit in the front seats of the car. This makes sense since either the father or the mother will be the drivers of the car, often times switching off the driving task from one to the other. In prior times the driving task was considered to be "manly" and so usually the husband was shown driving the car. In contemporary times, whatever the nature of and gender of the parents, the point is that the licensed driving adults are most likely to be seated in the front of the car.

If there are two parents, why have both in the front seat, you might ask? Couldn't you put one of the children up in the front passenger seat, next to the parent or adult that is driving the car? You can certainly arrange things that way, but the usual notion about having the front passenger be another adult or parent is that they can be watching the roadway, serving as an extra pair of eyes for the driver. The driver might be preoccupied with the traffic in front of the car, and meanwhile the front passenger notices that further up ahead there is a bridge-out sign warning that approaching cars need to be cautious. The front passenger is a kind of co-pilot, though they don't have ready access to the car controls and must instead verbally provide advice to the driver.

The front passenger is not always shown though in movies as a dispassionate observer that thoughtfully aids the driver. Humorous anecdotes are often shown as the front passenger suddenly points at a cow and screams out load for everyone to look. The driver could be distracted by such an exclamation and inadvertently drive off the road at the sudden yelling and pointing. Another commonly portrayed scenario is the front passenger that insists the driver take the next right turn ahead, but offering such a verbal instruction once the car is nearly past the available turn. The driver is then torn between making a radical and dangerous turn, or passing the turn entirely and then likely getting berated by the front seat passenger.

Does this seem familiar to you?

If so, you are likely a veteran of family road trips. Congratulations.

What about the children that are seated in the back seat of the car? One portrayal would be of young children with impressionable minds that are carefully studying their parents and learning the wise ways of life, doing so during the vacation and they will become more learned young adults because of the experience. Of course, this is not the stuff of reality.

Instead, the movies show something that pertains more closely to reality. The kids often feel trapped. Their parents are forcing them along on a trip. It's a trip the parents want, but not necessarily what the kids want. At times feeling like prisoners, they need to occupy themselves for hours at time on long stretches of highway. Though at first it might be keen to see an open highway and the mountains and blue skies, it is something that won't last your attention for hours upon hours, days upon days. Boredom sets in. Conversation with the parents also can only last so long. The parents are out-of-touch with the interests, musical tastes, and other facets of the younger generation.

The classic indication is that ultimately the kids will get into a fight. Not a fisticuffs fight per se, more like an arms waving and hands slapping kind of fight. And the parents then need to turn their heads and look at the kids with laser like eyes, and tell the kids in overtly stern terms, stop that fighting back there or it will be heck to pay. No more ice cream, no more allowance, or whatever other levers the parents can use to threaten the kids to behave. Don't make me come back there, is the usual refrain.

Sometimes one or more of the kids will start crying. Could be for just about any reason. They are tired of the trip and want it to end. They got hit by their brother or sister and want the parents to know so. Etc. The parents will often retort that the kids need to stop crying. Or, as they are want to say, they'll give them a true reason to cry (a veiled threat). If the kids are complaining incessantly about the trip, this will likely produce the other classic veiled threat of "I'd better not hear another peep out of you!"

Does the above suggest that the togetherness of the family road trip is perhaps hollow and we should abandon the pretense of having a family trip? I don't think so. It's more like showing how family trips really happen. In that sense, the movie National Lampoon's Vacation was a more apt portrayal than a Leave It To Beaver kind of portrayal, at least in more modern times.

Indeed, today's family road trips are replete with gadgets and electronics in the car. The kids are likely to be focusing on their smartphones and tablets. The car probably has WiFi, though at times only getting intermittent reception as the trip across some of the more barren parts of the United States takes place. There might be TV's built into the headrests so the kids can watch movies that way. One of the more popular and cynical portrayals of today's family road trips is that there is no actual human-to-human interaction inside the car, since everyone is tuned into their own electronic device.

Given the above description of how the family road trip seems to occur, what can we anticipate for the future?

First, it is important to point out that there are varying levels of self-driving cars. The topmost level, a level 5 self-driving car, consists of having AI that can drive the car without any human intervention. This means there is no need for a human driver. The AI should be able to do all of the driving, in the same manner that a human could drive the car. At the levels less than 5, there is and must be a human driver in the car. The self-driving car is not expected to be able to drive entirely on its own and relies upon having a human driver that is at-the-ready to take over the car controls.

For the levels less than 5, the AI self-driving car is essentially going to be a lot like a conventional car in terms of what happens during the family road trip. Admittedly, the human driver will be able to have a direct "co-pilot" of sorts to co-share in the driving task via the AI, but otherwise the car design is pretty much the same as a conventional car. This is because you need to have the human driver seated at the front of the car, and the human driver has to have access to car controls to then drive the car. With that essential premise, you can't otherwise change too much of the interior design of the car.

As an aside, there are some that have suggested maybe we don't need the human driver to be looking out the windshield and that we can change the car design accordingly. We could put the human driver in the back seat and have them wear a Virtual Reality headset and be connected to the controls of the car via some kind of handheld devices or foot-operated nearby devices. Cameras on the hood and top of the car would beam the visual images to the VR headset. Yes, I suppose this is all possible, but I really doubt we are going to see cars go in that direction. I would say it is a likelier bet that cars less than a level 5 will be designed to look like a conventional car, and only will the level 5 self-driving cars have a new design. We'll see.

For a level 5 self-driving car, since there is no need for a human driver, we can completely remake the interior of the car. No need to put a fixed place at the front of the car for the human driver to sit. No need for the human driver to look out the windshield. Some of the new designs suggest that one approach would be to have swivel seats for let's say four passengers in the normal sized self-driving car. The four swivel seats can be turned to face each other, allowing a togetherness of discussion and interaction. At other times, you can rotate the seats so that you have let's say two facing forward as though the front seats of the car, and the two behind those that are also facing forward.

Other ideas include allowing the seats to become beds. It could be that two seats can connect together and their backs be lowered, thus allowing for a bed, one that is essentially at the front of the car and another at the back of the car. Part of the reason that some are considering designing beds into an AI self-driving car is the belief that AI self-driving cars might be used 24x7, and people might sleep in their cars while on their way to work or while on their vacations.

Another design aspect involves lining the interior of the self-driving car with some kind of TV or LEDs that would allow for the interior to be a kind of movie theatre. This would allow for watching of movies, shows, live streaming, and even for doing online education. This also raises the question as to whether any kind of glass windows are needed at all. Some assert that we don't need windows anymore for a Level 5 self-driving car. Instead, the cameras on the outside of the car can show what would otherwise be seen if you looked out a window. The interior screens would show what the cameras show, unless you then wanted to watch a movie and thus the interior screens would switch to displaying that instead.

Are we really destined to have people sitting in self-driving car shells that have no actual windows? It seems somewhat farfetched. You would think that people will still want to look out a real window. You would think that people would want to be able roll down their window when they wish to do so. Now, you could of course have true windows and make the glass out of material that can become transparent at times, and then become blocked at other times, thus potentially have the best of both worlds. We'll see.

For a family road trip, you could configure the seats so that all four are facing each other, and have family discussions or play games or otherwise directly interact. This might not seem attractive to some people, or might be something that they sparingly do when trying to have a family chat. As mentioned, the seats could swivel to allow more of a conventional sense of privacy while sitting in your seat. I'd suggest though that the days of the parents saying don't make us come back there are probably numbered. The "there" will be the same place that the parents are sitting. Maybe too much togetherness? Or, maybe it will spark a renewal of togetherness?

Another factor to consider is that none of the human occupants needs to be a driver. In theory, a family road trip has always consisted of one or more drivers, and the rest were occupants. Now, everyone is going to be an occupant. Will parents feel less "useful" since they are no longer undertaking the driving task directly? Or, will parents find this a relief since they can use the time to interact with their children or catch-up on their reading or whatever?

This has another potentially profound impact on the family road trip, namely that no one needs to know how to drive a car. Thus, in theory, you could even have just and only the children in the self-driving car and have no parents or adults at all. I'd agree that this doesn't feel like a "family" trip at that point, but it could be that the parents are at the hotel and the kids want to go see the nearby theme park, and so the parents tell the kids they can take the self-driving car there.

How should the interior of the self-driving car be reshaped or re-designed if you have only children inside the car for lengths of time? Would there be interior aspects that you'd want to be able close off from use or slide away to be hidden from use? Perhaps you would not want the children to swivel the swivel seats and be able to lock in place the swivel seats during their journey. Via a Skype like communication capability, you would likely want to interact with the kids, they seeing you and you seeing them via cameras pointed inward into the self-driving car.

Without a human driver, the AI is expected to do all of the driving. When you go on a cross-country road trip, you often discover "hidden" places to visit that are remote and not on the normal beaten path. The question will be how good is the AI when confronted with driving in an area that perhaps no GPS exists per se. Driving on city roads that have been well mapped is one thing. Driving on dirt roads that are not mapped or for which no map is available, this can be a trickier aspect. Suppose too that you want to have the self-driving car purposely go off-road. The AI has to be able to do that kind of driving, assuming that there is no provision for a human driver and only the AI is able to drive the car.

An AI self-driving car at a Level 5 will normally have some form of Over-The-Air (OTA) capability. This allows the AI to get updated by the auto maker or tech firm, and also for the AI to report what is has discovered into the auto maker or tech firm cloud for collective learning purposes. On a cross country road trip, the odds are that there will be places that have no immediate electronic communication available. Suppose there's an urgent patch that the OTA needs to provide to the AI self-driving car? This can be dicey when doing a family road trip to off-road locations.

Suppose the family car, an AI self-driving car, suffers some kind of mechanical breakdown during the trip? What then? Keep in mind that a self-driving car is still a car. This means that parts can break or wear out. This means that you'll need to get the car to a repair shop. And, with the sophisticated sensors on an AI self-driving car, it will likely have more frequent breakdowns and will require more sophisticated repair specialists and cost more to be repaired. The road trip could be marred by not being able to find someone in a small town that can deal with your broken down AI self-driving car.

The AI of the self-driving car will become crucial as your driving "pilot" and companion, as it were. Take us to the next town, might be a command that the human occupants utter. One of the children might suddenly blurt out "I need to go to the bathroom" – in the olden days the parents would say hold it until you reach the next suitable place. What will the AI say? Presumably, if its good at what it does, it would have looked up where the next bathroom might be, and offer to stop there. This though is trickier than it seems. We cannot assume that the entire United States will be so well mapped that every bathroom can be looked up. The AI might need to be using its sensors to identify places that might appear to have a bathroom, in the same manner that a parent would furtively look at the window at a gas station or a rest stop.

There is also the possibility of using V2V (vehicle to vehicle communications) to augment the family road trip. With V2V, an AI self-driving car can potentially electronically communicate with another AI self-driving car. Maybe up ahead there is an AI self-driving car that has discovered that the paved road has large ruts and it is dangerous to drive there. This might be relayed to AI self-driving cars a mile back, so those AI self-driving cars can avoid the area or at least be prepared for what is coming. The AI of those self-driving cars could even warn the family (the human occupants) to be ready for a bumpy ride for the mile up ahead.

There is too the possibility of V2I (vehicle to infrastructure communications). This involves having the roadway infrastructure electronically communicate with the AI self-driving car. It could be that a bridge is being repaired, but you wouldn't know this from simply looking at a map. The bridge itself might be beaming out a signal that would forewarn cars within a few miles that the bridge is inoperable. Once again the AI self-driving car could thus re-plan the journey, and also warn the occupants about what's going on.

One aspect that the AI can provide that might or might not have been done by a parent would be to explain the historical significance and other useful facets about where you are. Have you been on a family road trip and researched the upcoming farm that was once run by a U.S. president, or maybe there's a museum where the first scoop of ice cream was ever dished out? A family road trip is often done to see and understand our heritage. What came before us? How did the country get formed? The AI can be a tour guide, in addition to driving the car.

As perhaps is evident, the interior of the self-driving car has numerous possibilities in terms of how it might be reshaped for the advent of true Level 5 AI self-driving cars. For a family road trip, the interior can hopefully foster togetherness, while also allowing for privacy. It might accommodate sleeping while driving from place to place. The AI will be the driver, and be guided by where the human occupants want to go. In addition to driving, the AI can be a tour guide and perform various other handy tasks too. This is not all rosy though, and the potential for lack of electronic communications could hamper the ride, along with the potential for mechanical breakdowns that might be hard to get repaired.

No more veiled threats from the front seats to the back seats. I suppose some other veiled threats will culturally develop to replace those. Maybe you tell the children, behave yourselves or I won't let you use the self-driving car to go to the theme park. Will we have AI self-driving cars possibly zipping along our byways with no adults present and only children, as they do a "family" road trip? That's a tough one to ponder for now. In any case, enjoy the family road trips of today, using a conventional car or even a self-driving car up to the level 5. Once we have level 5 AI self-driving cars, it will be a whole new kind of family road trip experience.

CHAPTER 5
AI DEVELOPER BURNOUT
AND
SELF-DRIVING CARS

CHAPTER 5

AI DEVELOPER BURNOUT AND SELF-DRIVING CARS

Did you realize that apparently more than half of all United States medical doctors are suffering from burnout?

You might at first glance not be overly surprised, since you've likely seen how harried most medical doctors are. Often, their patient load is at the max and they barely have time to say hello before they move onto the next patient. Many medical doctors bitterly complain that the nature of the healthcare system prevents them from spending quality time with their patients as they are under strict time guidelines and have little choice in the matter of how they use their time with patients.

You might also be thinking that it doesn't matter that medical doctors might be suffering burnout. The perception is that they are well-paid anyway, and so if they have to work long and hard hours, so be it. Some might think of them as whiners that don't realize how good they really have it. This though would be a misunderstanding about the impacts of burnout.

The medical doctors reported that nearly one in ten of them had committed a significant medical mistake, one or more such mistakes or errors, in the three-month period prior to the poll being taken. It is generally well proven already that burnout leads to medical doctors making mistakes or errors, and we now know the alarming frequency in which it can occur.

There can be errors in ascertaining the ailment that a patient has, or maybe a mistake in a prescription issued for a patient, and so on. The burnout therefore can directly and adversely impact the nature and quality of the healthcare provided to patients. In addition, medical doctors can become depressed, have high fatigue, and otherwise be less effective and efficient in performing their medical tasks.

Presumably, burnout is a reversible work-related matter.

If you can detect early enough that someone is suffering from burnout at work, you can potentially provide them guidance on how to alleviate the burnout. Some try stress management techniques to reduce their burnout. Some use the latest in so-called mindfulness training. Some try to seek a balance between the demands of work and their other life pursuits, carving out more time and attention to efforts outside work that enable them to better contend with the work situation.

It is usually unlikely that changes by the individual alone that has exhibited the burnout is going to be sufficient to curtail the burnout. The work situation often needs to also adjust. An organization has to realize what factors are leading to the burnout, and potentially readjust work schedules, or adjust the nature of the work being performed, and so on. Someone that is otherwise well prepared to contend with burnout is still going to have a tough time not getting burned out if the work environment that presumably is causing the burnout does not make adjustments too. It takes two to tango, as they say.

When I mention that burnout is potentially reversible, I'd like to clarify that for some people in some companies it is not reversible. When someone reaches a certain threshold, they can be so far gone that they cannot find within themselves the desire and nor the need to re-commit themselves to work, even if the company offers to try and find a means to do so. I've seen some workers that got burned out at a firm and they left in disgust and with no intention of ever returning. That being said, I've seen some firms that claimed they wanted to save someone that was burned out, but the firm did nothing more than token attempts to keep the person, which for that person made them even more determined to leave the firm.

When considering medical doctors that get burned out, you need to consider not just the impact on them and their patients, but also take a wider view and consider the larger ramifications. The odds are that if the patient gets less capable medical care due to the burn out, it might also indirectly impact their family and friends. Those family and friends might need to provide other outside care or additional care to make-up for whatever medical errors or omissions occur. The odds are that fellow staff at the medical facility will also suffer, having to either deal day-to-day with a medical doctor that might be difficult to deal with, or need to deal with patients that become irate when they realize they are not getting their desired care. Overall, you could make the claim that medical doctor burnout will raise costs overall for the medical delivery system and all of society accordingly, and also reduce the available medical care for others by needlessly consuming limited available medical resources by the burnout effects.

There are some workers that drive their own burnout. You've likely dealt with a workaholic that seems to work all of the time. They say that it makes them stronger and they enjoy it. This can sometimes be true, but more often than not it is the path towards burnout. A workaholic can work themselves to the bone. For some junior managers they think that having a workaholic under them is great, since the person gets so much work done. But, in the end, the person might be a prime candidate for burnout and thus the junior manager has likely done a disservice by not having done something about the matter earlier.

Besides the workaholic, there are other types of workers that can be especially susceptible to burnout. There's the lone ranger that tries to take on all the work themselves and doesn't appropriately make use of their fellow team mates. There's the perfectionist that wants to do everything to the nth degree and often goes overboard in terms of their work. There's the superhero type that relishes coming to the rescue on efforts and will become overwhelmed with work. There's the martyr that likes to do tons of work to be able to let others know that they are doing so. Etc.

Besides medical doctors, there are other professions that involve substantial amounts of burnout.

One such occupation are the AI developers that are working on AI self-driving cars.

At the Cybernetic AI Self-Driving Car Institute, we are developing AI software for self-driving cars and besides our own AI developers we also keep in touch with other self-driving car AI developers.

Generally, burn out is pervasive among such AI developers.

Why?

You might at first think that it would be an exciting and enjoyable job to be an AI developer for AI self-driving cars. It's like trying to achieve a moonshot and having been there in the early days of developing the Apollo spacecraft's that got us to the moon. There's a thrill about doing something that could change society. It has the potential for great benefits to all of us. That kind of a job should be joyous!

Though it is true that you could perceive the job as striving to achieve new ends and changing our lives, getting there is not all fun and games.

Let's consider why there is a high chance for burnout for AI developers that are developing AI self-driving cars:

• New Ground

AI self-driving cars are pushing the boundaries of what we can do with AI. This is not run-of-the-mill stuff. We are using the latest AI techniques, the latest Machine Learning (ML) capabilities, etc. Many everyday developers often just reuse what they have done before. In this case, it's new ground with every step you take.

- Life-or-Death System

It's one thing if you are pushing the boundaries of AI for let's say a financial system, but in the case of a self-driving car, it's a life-or-death matter. If your software hiccups at the wrong time, it could mean that the car will hurtle itself into a wall and kill the human occupants. Or, it could swerve unintentionally and kill pedestrians. And so on. This is serious stuff.

- Real-time System

Whenever you are developing software for a real-time system, it tends to increase the difficulty factor. One of the first real-time systems I was involved in, years ago, involved a real-time controller for a roller coaster. I can tell you that we sweated quite a bit about how to get the timing just right and make sure the software was always able to handle whatever happened in real-time.

- Intense Pressure

The pressure by the auto makers and tech firms to get their self-driving cars on the roadways is intense. Every day you see new announcements about one self-driving car maker is going to get to the market sooner than the other. This kind of gamesmanship is often taking place without regard to what the actual AI developers can do – it's about what they leaders are telling the marketplace. Deadlines aplenty. Irrational deadlines aplenty.

- Lack of Specs

Many of the auto makers and tech firms are developing their self-driving cars on-the-fly in an agile method and doing so without a definitive set of specs. To some degree, it's make it up as you go. Some of the ideas that are being delved into these projects are dreams rather than something that can be actually achieved. AI developers are often told, rather than asked, what can be done.

- Spotty Peer Expertise

There aren't many that have industrial style expertise in developing software for cars, let alone for AI self-driving cars. Thus, it is somewhat unlikely that an AI developer can depend upon their fellow AI developer on their team to lend a hand. The odds are that they are all mainly in-the-dark and trying to figure out things as they go along.

- Highly Secretive

The self-driving car efforts by each auto maker and tech firm are typically being done in a skunk works operation that's considered for secure eyes only. This secretive manner makes sense because everyone is trying to do their own thing and they don't want others to steal it. But, this also makes things harder for the AI developers since it narrows whom else they can turn to for assistance. In many cases, they aren't supposed to talk about their work with family and friends – it's like being in the CIA.

- Shift From R&D

For many of the AI developers in the self-driving cars field, they most recently were working at an AI research lab at a university. That's a whole different kind of work environment than in industry. For example, at a university, there is often the view that failing on something is OK since you are doing experimentation and not everything will work out. No matter what you hear about Silicon Valley saying to fail first and fail fast, I assure you that with the pressures to get self-driving cars going, the "let's try failing" model is verboten.

- Long Hours

With the vast amount of work to be done for the AI of a self-driving car, there are long hours involved. It can be frustrating too because as mentioned it is punctuated with trying new things and hoping they will work. And, you can't readily explain to family and friends why you are working late and on the weekends, other than they know vaguely you are working on something important and hush-hush.

- Other

There are a myriad of other factors involved too. For example, even the tools used to develop the AI systems are at times brittle and still untried. It would be like trying to make a house and you have hammers and screwdrivers that no one knows for sure will work properly.

Now, I realize that many of these AI developers are getting paid big bucks. As such, similar to the perception about medical doctors, you might have little sympathy about these AI developers possibly getting burned out. You might say they should relish their moment in the sun. Now's the time to make enough bucks to then retire.

Well, maybe, but let's also consider the impacts of burnout, similar to the concerns when medical doctors experience burnout.

In the case of the AI self-driving cars, it can lead to the AI developers making errors or mistakes, more likely than they might have otherwise. Perhaps mistakes are made in the machine learning and so the AI system is unable to properly interpret a road sign. Or, perhaps there's a bug in the code that when the self-driving car reaches a particular speed that the code burps and gets stuck in a loop that it can't get out of.

Here's the major actions that an AI self-driving car undertakes:
- Sensor data collection and interpretation
- Sensor fusion
- Virtual World model updating
- AI Action Plan updating
- Cars control commands issuance

A burned out AI developer can be "lazy" when it comes to testing and decide that they've done too much testing already. Or, they might have an attitude of "why test it" since they don't believe the whole thing will work anyway. Or, they might fix something that they find as broken, and in the effort of rendering the fix they inadvertently and unknowingly introduce another problem into the code.

Of course, any of these aspects can happen to any developer. And they do. But, as mentioned earlier, it is magnified in the case of AI developers for self-driving cars due to the pressures involved, and the pushing of new boundaries, and so on. Plus, this is a real-time system that involves life-and-death aspects. Thus, this happening for AI developers of self-driving cars has especially important and significant ramifications.

Imagine the problems of AI code that is half-hearted and does the sensor data collection interpretation. Or that does the sensor fusion. Or that does the virtual world modeling. Or that does the AI action plan updating. Or that does the cars control commands issuance. What also can hamper things is that an error in one of those crucial components can compound itself by then misleading the other components. It can have an adverse cascading impact. This includes the potential for the Freezing Robot Problem.

What can be done about the burnout of AI developers that are creating the next generation of self-driving cars?

First, it's vital to acknowledge that the burnout can and does exist. There are some firms that are blind to burnout and don't know it happens. They often just say that Joe or Samantha need to take a day off, and when they get back they'll be fine again. This kind of Band-Aid approach fails to recognize the depth and seriousness of true burnout, and the lengthy and complex process to typically undo it.

Next, watch out for the burnout culture that some firms seem to foster. I say this because there are many Silicon Valley firms that actually tout their burnout rates. They like to chew-up people. They make it into a macho kind of atmosphere and try to project an image that only the strong survive. In their viewpoint, if you aren't already on the verge of burnout, get there or get out. I've been waiting to see what happens when those employees so treated decide to finally lawyer-up and go after those firms for the cruddy work environment. We'll see.

In some firms, they buy a ping pong table or a foosball table and that's their way of telling the employees to not burnout. Somehow, you are supposed to take time off from your non-stop high-pressure AI development work, and by playing ping pong a few times a day you'll not get burned out. Doubtful.

Firms that are serious about detecting, mitigating, and preventing burnout will go out of their way to try and arrange the nature of the work and the work situations to deal with burnout. They need to hire the right people, put in place the right managers, provide the right kind of leadership, and otherwise aim to gauge how much work can be reasonably done and by whom. There are many key decisions being made about self-driving car designs, and the coding, which will either aid the fulfillment of self-driving cars, or will have the opposite impact and completely undermine the advent of self-driving cars.

Some say that burnout in the workplace leads to the erosion of the soul. I know one promising AI developer that nearly collapsed at the pace that he was going, and decided that it was just too unhealthy to continue on this kind of work. He's since switched to another occupation entirely. That's a shame as we already have too few well-qualified AI developers to start with. And we need a lot more of them to ramp up for achieving a true Level 5 self-driving car.

I've seen some AI developers that have emotional exhaustion from work burnout. One that went home and took it out on his wife and kids. Another one that became so cynical that he pretty much was approving any kind of code going into production. He had lost the belief in caring for his work. Now, you might say that there should be double-checks to catch these kinds of things in terms of faulty designs and faulty code, but with the go-go atmosphere and high pressures to produce, there are developers that look the other way and figure that it's up to the other person to make sure their stuff works properly.

I had mentioned earlier that if a medical doctor makes mistakes due to burnout, the patient suffers and also so do a lot of other stakeholders. The same can be said of the AI developers for self-driving cars. They can each in their own way lead to self-driving cars that just aren't ready for prime time. Unfortunately, those at the upper levels of an auto maker or tech firm might not know or care to know, and just insist that the self-driving car be put onto our roadways. If those self-driving cars harm humans, it's bad and it will also produce a backlash against self-driving cars overall.

And if that happens, if we have haywire AI that stop or stunts the advent of self-driving cars, it undermines or delays the potential benefits to society that we're all hoping that self-driving cars will derive. Thus, in that manner, even just one burnout can be like the butterfly that flaps its wings on one side of the earth and it ultimately leads to being felt on the other side of the globe.

I implore the auto makers and tech firms to carefully do an assessment of how they are treating their AI developers, and if it's "burnout city" then they would be wise to step-back, take another look, and see what can be done to overcome it. All of us need to watch out for that last straw on the camel's back that will break the spirit of our most prized workers, those AI developers, tasked with creating the future of society via the advent of self-driving cars.

CHAPTER 6

STEALING SECRETS ABOUT ABOUT SELF-DRIVING CARS

CHAPTER 6

STEALING SECRETS
ABOUT SELF-DRIVING CARS

Apple's self-driving car project is so cloaked in secrecy that most Apple employees know nothing about it. Lots of people all across the world would love to know what's going on in the skunk works of the Apple AI self-driving car efforts. Will Apple be the one that surprises us all and gets to a true Level 5 self-driving car before anyone else does? Will they shock the world and pull a rabbit out of hat? Or are they really only working on the next iPod? Nobody really can say, other than those sworn to secrecy.

Recently, a former Apple hardware engineer was busted for allegedly walking out the door with inner sanctum secrets about Apple's AI self-driving car project. In a story line suitable for a movie, the engineer was arrested while trying to get on a flight to China at the San Jose, California airport. A criminal complaint was filed in federal court and indicated that he allegedly downloaded numerous technical materials about the Apple self-driving car systems being designed and developed.

The reported background is that he had taken a paternity leave, came back to work afterward and said he would be leaving Apple, wanting to move back to China to aid his ailing mother. Meanwhile, apparently Apple's forensic analysis ascertained that his network activity at work had increased "exponentially" and he was also shown as entering the super-secret AI lab for the self-driving car operations via recorded closed-circuit video. He supposedly walked out with a server and circuit boards. And, he supposedly transferred Apple's confidential files to his wife's laptop. In his own defense, he allegedly said that he had merely wanted to study the materials on his own time, and then also apparently added that he was hopeful of getting a job at the self-driving car company XMotors.

Based on the criminal charges so far leveled against him, he's looking at a potential 10-year prison term and financial fines into the hundreds of thousands of dollars.

Let's move away from that instance and consider more broadly the notion that AI self-driving cars are hot right now, and the competition is fierce, and that it is quite likely that industrial espionage is going on, which can also spill over into outright thievery of secrets.

There's a famous notion that every day of an auto maker or tech firm their most precious secrets are walking out the door at the end of the work day, due to the self-driving car development knowledge in the minds of their AI workers. Of course, it's one thing for skilled workers to know their craft and be able to use the latest algorithms and machine learning techniques and tools, and it's another that they opt to reuse the specifics of a particular company elsewhere.

Many of the auto makers and tech firms try to limit what an AI developer can do if they leave the firm. Efforts to use non-compete clauses can be difficult to enforce, and in some states like California it's quite unlikely to have one with much teeth. You can't readily stop someone else from using their own base of skills and knowledge for other firms. Where things cross the line is when they try to use the specifics of something considered proprietary from the firm that they were once with.

What makes these kinds of reuses even more brazen and into the illegal zone is when someone takes stuff from their employer. Taking home a server, that's pretty gutsy. Downloading thousands of lines of Python and C++ code, unless you have a bona fide reason, it's going to get a lot of scrutiny. Grabbing terabytes of data used to train that machine learning system being used to help guide a self-driving car, well it's questionable. And so on.

You might remember the lawsuit of Waymo against Uber when there had been accusations that a former Waymo employee downloaded some 14,000 or so files of self-driving car designs from Waymo, including especially about their LIDAR devices, and he allegedly took it with him to Uber. It is said that Waymo had not known that the accused had done the download per se, at first, and were awakened to the possibility when they discovered later on an Uber LIDAR circuit board that looked a lot like their own.

The whole story became front-page news. Two titans squaring off over the latest in AI self-driving cars. In the end, Uber opted to pay Waymo about $245 million, and the two companies supposedly kissed and made-up. It was suggested that they see each other not as rivals, but instead as partners. The settlement avoided a lengthy and exposing trial. There are still chances though of other legal fallout arising from the matter.

The stories you are hearing about are just the tip of the iceberg. There is a humungous amount of "spying" going on in the AI self-driving car field and it's become almost like a CIA effort of trying to protect secrets. Firms are buying a competitor's self-driving car and tearing it down to the bones to figure out how it works. Company X offers a big bonus to lure away an AI developer from auto maker Y in order to try and do a leapfrog on the high-tech needed for self-driving cars they are developing. It's a dog eat dog world, for sure.

At the Cybernetic AI Self-Driving Car Institute, we are developing AI software for self-driving cars, and we find that it is a continual and overarching matter to keep our stuff safe and away from prying eyes.

It's almost as though lines of AI code or a particular neural network model and its neural weights and configuration are worth gold, or maybe pricy bitcoins, for those seeking to get an edge on the advent of AI self-driving cars. The major auto makers and tech firms are embroiled in an intense race to see who can get to the AI self-driving car first. It is perceived that whomever makes it first will grab the market and leave just crumbs for the rest.

If you watch the stock market, you'll see that each time a major auto maker or tech firm makes an announcement about their brewing new AI self-driving car, it causes their stock to either fly high or drop like a rock. The market is expecting that there will be wondrous self-driving cars arising pronto. The market rewards those that seem to be showcasing that story, and are quick to penalize those that don't.

What is it that everyone seems to want to find out about the other?

Consider that there are these major stages of an AI self-driving car's processing:
- Sensor data collection and interpretation
- Sensor fusion
- Virtual world model updating
- AI action plan formulation
- Car controls commands issuance

Imagine you are an auto maker that is struggling with getting the cameras and radar to properly identify street signs, which is part of the sensor data collection and interpretation processing. You've hired lots of AI developers, but they can't seem to get it to work. You begin to realize or assume that your firm is falling behind the others. What can you do? Try to hire someone from a competing firm and have them hopefully be able to innocently turnaround your efforts by their own base set of skills? Or, maybe have them apply what they specifically learned at the other firm? Or, maybe they bring with them some tried-and-true code that you can just insert into your system.

The person wanting to make a move to another firm might be wondering how can they best portray their capabilities to entice that other firm to hire them. Yes, they might have basic skills, but to reinvent the proverbial wheel from scratch at the other firm, well that's maybe a tall order. If they just grab ahold of some designs and other files, it would seem to make them an even more attractive addition.

Of course, these kinds of activities can swerve quickly into illegal acts. There can be hefty civil repercussions. There can be criminal repercussions. Some might be willing to take the risks, figuring that nobody will be able to trace what they did. Or, they figure take a chance, make some big bucks, and then use it as a defense fund to fight against any charges. They also often figure that firms might not want the adverse public relations blowout from airing the industry dirty laundry, thus, maybe the whole thing stays under the public radar.

Much of what we've seen so far in the AI self-driving car industry involves "insider" kinds of thefts. A contractor working for a company opts to take various technical materials with them and offer it to a competitor, or use it to get themselves an employee position at a competitor. Or, an employee of a firm that is wanting to get a job elsewhere takes with them some downloaded stuff. It could also be a partner firm, maybe an auto maker or tech firm contracts with a third-party to do some ancillary programming, and that so-called partner firm sneaks out some stuff that they figure could have other market value on the down-low.

Sometimes, it's an employee of a company that is doing self-driving car efforts but the employee has no direct involvement in the self-driving car project. This kind of employee feels distant from the project and often has some lesser paying role in another part of the firm. They vaguely know that the self-driving project is top secret and worth a lot of money. They then use their internal employee access to take whatever they can grab. They don't really even know what's what. They just hope that any digital assets they can find will be worth something. It's a wild fishing expedition.

Someone in-the-know might realize that the structure of the virtual world model is sorely sought by competitor Z. Or, they might have been approached about how they were able to solve problems of creating on-the-fly and in-real-time AI action plans for the driving task, and maybe they weren't directly involved in that aspect, but they snatch what they can, based on their insider access, study it and keep it around so that if they can jump over to the other firm they'll look like a superhero for solving their difficult programming challenges.

We haven't yet seen many of the external thievery that you'd expect to see.

For example, an individual that is outside the firm, and finds a method to "hack" into a company making an AI self-driving car. They then post online some designs or code, doing so for bragging rights of what they accomplished. I'm also anticipating that if self-driving cars continue to get in the news for harming people, we might see vigilante style attacks wherein an individual crack's into the files of a self-driving car company and posts it for the world to see. They are doing so as a social mission, in their mind, of letting the public know what's on the inside of these AI systems.

We've also not yet visibly seen poaching on a grander scale, such as a country that wants to get ahead in the AI self-driving car realm and so uses their state-funded cyber-hacking capabilities to try and get what they can from companies in other countries. I dare say that the auto makers and tech firms are all under continual cyber-attack by outsiders that are trying to get what they can break into. But, it doesn't seem to have yet risen to the country level, or at least not to the degree that it has been publicly disclosed. Once AI self-driving cars truly start to get into the marketplace, I'm betting we'll see more big actors that try these kinds of large-scale grabs.

You might say that the auto makers and tech firms should just be patenting their stuff and thus go after anyone that manages to somehow make the same thing. This is certainly one form of legal protection. For some of the auto makers and tech firms, they are actually holding back on filing for patents since they perceive that they don't want to divulge yet what they have. Their view is that to get to the market sooner, it's better for them to keep things proprietary and not reveal what they have, perhaps staving off the rest of the market from being able to catch-up.

What can an AI self-driving car company do to try and protect their secrets?

First, they need to put in place the various physical controls that are part-and-parcel for any kind of secretive operation. I had worked in the aerospace industry at the start of my career, and they knew how to put in place good physical controls. Restricted access. Employee badges. Man-traps. You name it.

That's not so easy to do in today's age. You've got the Silicon Valley culture that wants to be open and fun, which tends to clash with creating a work environment that seems like Fort Knox. It can be a tough balance to try and put in place physical controls that don't also cause your AI developers to feel like they are working in a prison. I did work at one firm that had no employee badges, they allowed anyone to wander anywhere once you got past the front lobby (which required no actual verification of identify or purpose), and was about as unguarded as you could imagine. An easy treasure trove for a self-driving car AI thief.

There's the importance of putting your online materials under digital lock-and-key. This requires some savvy cyber-security systems. It requires training the teams on how to watch out for phishing scams and other ways to break-in. Once again, it has to be hard enough to stop or slow down someone that wants to steal, but not be so onerous that the day-to-day developers get frustrated.

It's also a tough thing to tell your own employees that the protections are as much to prevent outsiders as it is to prevent insiders from taking things. This can be a slap in the face to many of the AI developers that are used to a more open and trusting environment, such as having come from a university research lab. There was a recent study that found that most professors and university research labs are readily susceptible to online scams and security break-ins. This makes sense because most of those environments and the mindset involve wanting to share new knowledge for the sake of advancing new innovations. They don't do much to protect what they have.

Auto makers and tech firms that are spending millions upon millions of dollars on their AI systems for self-driving cars are more motivated to keep what they have and try to prevent it from being taken.

Oddly, many of these firms though aren't spending as much on the computer security protections as they should. I liken this to the nature of earthquakes. Most people won't spend money on earthquake insurance or other earthquake protections, and only do so when a major earthquake comes along.

Similarly, until we have a big leak of some prominent AI self-driving car secrets, most firms will only be taking relatively token protective measures.

There's another perspective on the secrets stealing topic. Besides trying to prevent the stealing, the other aspect involves discovering when the secrets have been stolen. Some say that's like discovering that the horse is already out of the barn, and you should have done things to keep the horse in the barn to begin with. But, realistically, no matter what you do, you might as well realize that somehow someway the horse might get out. If so, you need to also try and discover so, as soon as possible, and be prepared as to handle it once you discover it is gone.

This detection or discovery is often aided by having various auditing tools on your network.

You need to be reviewing your logs.

You need to be overseeing the physical controls to try and ascertain if something is going out your doors.

There's also the watching of your competitors to see if they suddenly come forth with remarkably something identical to what you have. And, there are some that monitor the dark web, looking to see if anyone might be selling their AI self-driving car secrets.

I've spoken at self-driving car industry conferences, and when I mention this topic of being careful about your code and designs, I've had some tell me that it seems a bit paranoid.

There's the old line that it's not paranoia if there is really someone trying to come after you. I assure you, there are many that would like to take the "easy street" of getting your AI self-driving car specifications, codes, algorithms, machine learning models, designs, and all the rest, if they could do so, and turn it into their own gravy train. Better to be safe than sorry.

CHAPTER 7

AFFORDABILITY
AND SELF-DRIVING CARS

CHAPTER 7

AFFORDABILITY
AND SELF-DRIVING CARS

They'll cost too much. They will only be for the elite. Having one will be a sign of prestige. It's a rich person's toy. The "have nots" will not be able to get one. People are going to rise-up in resentment that the general population can't get one. Maybe the government should step in and control the pricing. Refuse to get into one as a form of protest. Ban them because if the rest of us cannot have one, nobody should.

What's this all about?

It's some of the comments that are already being voiced about the potential affordability (or lack thereof) of AI self-driving cars.

At the Cybernetic AI Self-Driving Car Institute, we are developing AI software for self-driving cars, and we get asked quite frequently about whether AI self-driving cars will be affordable or not. I thought you might find of interest my answer (read on).

When people clamor about the potential sky reaching cost of AI self-driving cars, you might at first wonder if people are maybe talking about flying cars, rather than AI self-driving cars. I mention this because there are some that say that flying cars will be very pricy and I think we all pretty much accept that notion. We know that jet planes are pricey, so why shouldn't a flying car be pricey. But, an earth-based car that rolls on the ground and cannot fly in the air, nor can it submerge like a submarine, we openly question how much such a seemingly "ordinary" car should cost.

It is said that a Rolls-Royce Sweptail is priced upwards of $13 million dollars. Have there been mass protests about this? Are we upset that only a few that are wealthy can afford such a car? Not really. It is pretty much taken for granted that there are cars that are indeed very expensive. Of course, we might all consider it rather foolish of those that are willing to pump hard-earned millions of dollars into such a car. We might think them pretentious for doing so. Or, we might envy them that they have the means to buy such a car. Either way, the Rolls-Royce and other such top to-end cars are over-the-top pricey and most people not especially complain or argue about it.

Part of the reason that people seem to object to the possible high price tag on an AI self-driving car is that the AI self-driving car is being touted as a means to benefit society. AI self-driving cars are ultimately hopefully going to cut down on the number of annual driving related deaths. AI self-driving cars will provide mobility to those that need it, and that cannot otherwise achieve it, such as the poor and the elderly. If an AI self-driving car has such tremendous societal benefits, then we want to as a society ensure that society as a whole gets those benefits and that those benefits will presumably apply across the board. It's a car of the people, for the people.

What kind of pricing then, for an AI self-driving car, are people apparently thinking of? Some that don't have any clue of what the price might be are leaving the price tag unknown and thus it makes things easier to get into a lather about how expensive it is. It could be a zillion dollars. Or more. This though seems like a rather vacuous way to discuss the topic. It would seem that we might be better off if we start tossing around some actual numbers and then see if that's prohibitive or not to buy an AI self-driving car.

The average transaction price (ATP) for a traditional passenger car in the United States for this year is so far around $36,000 according to various published statistics. That's the national average.

When AI self-driving cars first get started a few years ago, the cost of the added sensors and other specialized gear for achieving self-driving capabilities was estimated at somewhere around $100,000. Meanwhile, since then, the price on those self-driving car specialized components aspects has steadily come down. As with most high-tech, the cost starts "high" and then as it is perfected and the costs to make it wringed out of the process, the price heads downward. In any case, some at the time were saying that an AI self-driving car might be around $150,000 to $200,000, though that's a wild guess and we don't yet know what the real pricing will be. Will it be a million dollars for an AI self-driving car? That doesn't seem to be in anyone's estimates at this time.

Of course, any time a new car comes out, particularly one that has new innovations, there is usually a premium price placed on the car. It's a novelty item at first. The number of such cars is usually scarce initially, and so the usual laws of supply and demand help to punch up the price. If the car is able to be eventually mass produced, gradually the price starts to come down as more of those cars enter into the marketplace. If there are competitors that provide equivalent alternatives, the competition of the marketplace tends to drive down the price. You can refer to the Tesla models as prime examples of this kind of marketplace phenomena.

Suppose indeed that the first true AI self-driving cars in the low hundreds of thousands of dollars. Does that mean that those cars are out of the reach of the everyday person?

Before we jump into the answer for that question, let's clarify what I mean by true AI self-driving cars. There are levels of self-driving cars. The topmost level is Level 5. A Level 5 AI self-driving car is able to be driven by the AI without any human intervention. In fact, there is not a human driver needed in a Level 5 car. So much so that there is unlikely to be any driving controls in a Level 5 self-driving car for a human to operate even if the human wanted to try and drive it. In theory, the AI of the Level 5 self-driving car is supposed to be able to drive the car as a human could.

Let's therefore not consider in this affordability discussion the AI self-driving cars that are less than a Level 5. A less than level 5 self-driving car is a lot like a conventional car, though augmented in a manner that allows for co-sharing of the driving task. This means that there must be a human driver in a car that is classified as a less than Level 5 self-driving car. In spite of having whatever kind of AI in such a self-driving car, the driving task is still considered the responsibility of the human driver. No matter whether the human driver opts to take their eyes off the road, which can be an easy trap to fall into when in a less than level 5 self-driving car, and if the AI were to suddenly toss the control aspects to that human driver, it is nonetheless the human driver considered to be responsible for the driving. I've warned many times about the dangers this creates in the driving task.

We'll focus herein on the true Level 5 self-driving car. This is the self-driving car that has the full bells and whistles and really is a self-driving car. No human driver needed. This is the one that those referring to a driving utopia are actually meaning to bring up. The less than level 5's aren't quite so exciting, though they might well be important and perhaps stepping stones to the level 5.

Now, let's get back to the question at hand – will a true Level 5 AI self-driving car be affordable?

We can first quibble about the word "affordable" in this context. If by affordability we mean that it should be around the same price tag as the ATP $36,000 of today's average passenger car in the United States, I'd say that we aren't going to see Level 5 Ai self-driving cars at that price for likely a long time until after they are quite prevalent. In other words, out the gate, it isn't going to be that kind of price (it will be much higher). After years of growth of more and more AI self-driving cars coming into the marketplace, sure, it could possibly eventually come down to that range. Keep in mind that today there are around 200 million conventional cars in the United States, and presumably over time those cars will get replaced by AI self-driving cars. It won't happen overnight. It will be a gradual wind down of the old ways, and a gradual wind-up of the new ways.

Imagine that the first sets of AI self-driving cars will cost in the neighborhood of several hundreds of thousands of dollars. Obviously, that price is outside the range of the average person. No argument there.

But, that's if you only look at the problem or question in just one simple way, namely purchasing the car for purely personal use. That's the mental trap that most fall into. They perceive of the AI self-driving car as a personal car and nothing more. I'd suggest you reconsider that notion.

It is generally predicted and accepted that AI self-driving cars are likely to be running 24x7. You can have your self-driving car going all the time, pretty much. Today's conventional cars are only used around 5% of their available time. This makes sense because you drive your personal car to work, you park it, you work all day, you drive home. Over ninety percent of the day it is sitting and not doing anything other than being a paperweight, if you will.

For AI self-driving cars, you have an electronic chauffeur that will drive the car whenever you want. But, are you actually going to want to be going in your AI self-driving car all day long? I doubt it. So, you will have extra available driving capacity that is unused. You could just chock it up and say that's the way the ball bounces. More than likely, you would realize that you could turn that idle time into personal revenue.

Here's what is most likely to actually happen.

We all generally agree that the advent of the AI self-driving car will spur the ridesharing industry. In fact, some say that the AI self-driving car will shift our society into a ridesharing-as-an-economy model. This is why the Uber and Lyft and other existing ridesharing firms are so frantic about AI self-driving cars. Right now, ridesharing firms are able to justify what they do because they are able to connect together human drivers with cars to those that need a lift. If you eliminate the human driver out of the equation, what then if the ridesharing firm doing? That's the scary proposition for the ridesharing firms.

This all implies that ridesharing-as-a-service will now be possible by the masses. It doesn't matter if you have a full-time job and cannot spare the time to be a ridesharing driver, because instead you just let your AI self-driving car be your ridesharing service. You mainly need to get connected up with people that need a ridesharing lift. How will that occur? Uber and Lyft are hopeful it will occur via their platform, but it could instead be say a Facebook wherein the people are already there in the billions. This is all going to be a big shakeout coming.

Meanwhile, you buy yourself an AI self-driving car, and you use it for some portion of the time, and the rest of the time you have it earning some extra dough as a ridesharing vehicle. Nice!

This then ties into the affordability question posed earlier.

If you are going to have revenue generated by your AI self-driving car, you can then look at it as a small business of sorts. You then should consider your AI self-driving car as an investment. You are making an investment in an asset that you can put to work and earn revenue. As such, you should then consider what the revenue might be and what the cost might be to achieve that revenue.

This opens the door towards being able to afford an otherwise seemingly unaffordable car. Even if the AI self-driving car costs you say several hundreds of thousands of dollars, which seems doubtful as a price tag, but let's use it as an example, you can weigh against that the revenue you can earn from that car.

For tax purposes (depending on how taxes will be regulated in the era of AI self-driving cars), you can usually deduct a car loan interest when using a car for business purposes (the deduction is only with respect to the portion of it used for business purposes). So, suppose you use your AI self-driving car for 15% of the time, and the other 85% of the time you use it for your ridesharing business, you can deduct the car loan interest normally for the 85% portion.

You can also do deductions for tax purposes, sometimes using the federal standard mileage rate, or also with actual vehicle expenses including:

- Depreciation
- Licenses
- Gas and oil
- Tolls
- Lease payments
- Insurance
- Garage rent
- Parking fees
- Registration fees
- Repairs
- Tires

Therefore, you need to rethink the cost of an AI self-driving car. It becomes a potential money maker and you need to consider the cost to purchase the car, the cost of ongoing maintenance and support, the cost of special taxes, the cost of undertaking the ridesharing services, and other such associated costs.

These costs are weighed in comparison to the potential revenue. You might at first only be thinking of the revenue derived from the riders that use your AI self-driving car. You might also consider that there is the opportunity for in-car entertainment that you could possibly charge a fee for (access to streaming movies, etc.), perhaps in-car provided food (you might stock the self-driving car with a small refrigerator and have other food in it), etc. You can also possibly use your AI self-driving car for doing advertising and get money from advertisers based on how many eyeballs see their ads while people are going around in your AI self-driving car.

And, this all then becomes part of your budding small business. You get various tax breaks. You might also then expand your business into other areas of related operations or even beyond AI self-driving cars entirely.

One related tie-in might be with the companies that are providing ridesharing scooters and bicycles. Suppose someone gets into your AI self-driving car and they indicate that when they reach their destination, they'd like to have a bicycle to rent. Your ridesharing service might have an arrangement with a firm that does those kinds of ridesharing services, and you get a piece of the action accordingly.

Will the average person be ready to be their own AI self-driving car mogul?

Likely not. But, fear not, a cottage industry will quickly arise that will support the emergence of small businesses that are doing ridesharing with AI self-driving cars. I'll bet there will be seminars on how to setup your own corporation for these purposes. How to keep your ridesharing AI self-driving car always on the go. Accountants will promote their tax services to the ridesharing start-ups. There will be auto maintenance and repair shops that will seek to be your primary go-to for keeping your ridesharing money maker going. And so on.

In that sense, there will be a ridesharing-as-a-business business that booms to help new entrepreneurs on how to tap into the ridesharing-as-a-service economy. Make millions off your AI self-driving car, will be the late night TV infomercials. You'll see ads on YouTube of a smiling person that says until they got their AI self-driving car they were stuck in a dead-end job, but now, with their money producing AI self-driving car, they are so wealthy they don't know where to put all the money they are making. The big bonanza is on its way.

This approach of being a solo entrepreneur to afford an AI self-driving car is only one of several possible approaches. I'd guess it will be perhaps the most popular.

I'll caution though that it is not a guaranteed path to riches. There will be some that manage to get themselves an AI self-driving car and then discover that it is not being put to ridesharing use as much as they thought. It could be that they live in an area swamped with other AI self-driving cars and so they get just leftover crumbs of ridesharing requests. Or, they are in an area that has other mass transit and no one needs ridesharing. Or, maybe few will trust using an AI self-driving car and so there won't be many that are willing to use it for ridesharing. Another angle is that you get such a car and do so under the assumption it will be ridesharing for 85% of the time, but you instead use it for personal purposes 70% of the time and this leaves only 30% of the time for the ridesharing (cutting down on the revenue potential).

Meanwhile, there are some other alternatives, let's briefly consider them:

- Solo ridesharing business as a money maker (discussed so far) of an AI self-driving car
- Pooling an AI self-driving car
- Timeshare an AI self-driving car
- Personal use exclusively of an AI self-driving car
- Other

In the case of pooling an AI self-driving car, imagine that your next door neighbor would like an AI self-driving car and so would you. The two of you realize that since the neighbor starts work at 7 a.m., while you start work at 8 a.m., and the kids of both families start school at 9 a.m., here's what you could do. You and the neighbor split the cost of an AI self-driving car. It takes your neighbor to work at 7 a.m., comes back and takes you to work at 8 a.m., comes back and takes the kids to school by 9 a.m. In essence, you all pool the use of the AI self-driving car. There's no revenue aspects, it's all just being used for personal use, on a group basis. This could be done with more than just one neighbor.

The pooling would then allow you to split the cost of the AI self-driving car, making it more affordable per person. Suppose you have 3 people and they decided to evenly split the cost, this would make it so that you'd only need to afford one-third of whatever the prevailing cost would be of an AI self-driving car at that time. Voila, the cost is less, seemingly so. But, you'd need to figure out the sharing aspects and I realize it could get heated as to who gets to use the AI self-driving car when needed. It's like having only one TV and it might be difficult at times to balance the aspect that someone wants to watch one show and someone else wants another one – say you need the AI self-driving car to take you to the store, while the kids need it to get to the ballpark.

In the case of the timeshare approach, you buy into an AI self-driving car like you would if buying into a condo in San Carlo. You purchase a time-based portion of the AI self-driving car. You can use it for whatever is the agreed amount of time. Potentially, you can opt to "invest" in more than one at a time, perhaps getting a timeshare in a passenger car that's an AI self-driving car, and also investing in an RV that's an AI self-driving vehicle.

You would use them each at different times for their suitable purposes. With any kind of timesharing arrangement, watch out for the details and whether you can get out of it or it might have other such limitations.

There's the purely personal use of an AI self-driving car option too, which we started this discussion by saying it might be too much for the average person to afford. Even that is somewhat malleable in that there are likely to be car loans that take into account that you are buying an AI self-driving car. The loans might be very affordable in the sense that there's the collateral of the car, plus the AI self-driving car if needed can be repossessed and then turned into a potential money maker.

The auto makers and the banks and others might be willing to cut some pretty good loans to get you into your very own AI self-driving car. As always, watch out for the interest and any onerous loan terms!

Well, before we get too far ahead of ourselves, the main point to be made is that even if AI self-driving cars are priced "high" in comparison to today's conventional cars, it does not necessarily mean that those AI self-driving cars are only going to be only for the very rich.

Instead, those AI self-driving cars are actually going to be a means to help augment the wealth of those that see this as an opportunity. Not everyone will be ready or willing to go the small business route. For many, it will be a means to not only enjoy the benefits of AI self-driving cars, but also spark them towards becoming entrepreneurs. Let's see how this all plays out and maybe it adds another potential benefit to the emergence of AI self-driving cars.

CHAPTER 8
CROSSING THE RUBICON
AND
SELF-DRIVING CARS

CHAPTER 8

CROSSING THE RUBICON
AND SELF-DRIVING CARS

Julius Caesar is famously known for his radical act in 49 BC of defying authority by marching his army across the Rubicon river. Unless you happen to be a historian, you might not be aware that the Roman Senate had explicitly ordered Caesar to disband his army, return to Rome, and not to bring his troops across the Rubicon. His doing so was an outright act of defiance.

Not only was Caesar defiant, he was risking everything by taking such a bold and unimaginable act. The government of Rome and its laws were very clear cut that that any imperium (a person appointed with the right to command) that dared to cross the Rubicon would forfeit their imperium, meaning they would no longer hold the right to command troops. Furthermore, it was considered a capital offense that would cause the commander to become an outlaw. The commander would be condemned to death, and -- just to give the commander some pause for thought, all of the troops that followed the commander across the Rubicon would also be condemned to death. Presumably, the troops would not be willing to risk their own lives, even if the commander was willing to risk his life.

As we now know, Caesar made the crossing. When he did so, he reportedly exclaimed "alea iacta est" which loosely translated means that the die has been cast. We use today the idiom "crossing the Rubicon" to suggest a circumstance where you've opted to go beyond a point of no return. There is no crossing back. You can't undo what you've done. In the case of Caesar, his gamble ultimately paid-off, and he was never punished, and he led the Roman Empire, doing so until his assassination in 44 BC.

I'm sure that most of us have had situations where we felt like we were crossing the Rubicon. One time I was out in the wilderness as a scout master and decided to take the scouts over to a mountain area that was readily hiked over to. While doing the hike, I began to realize that we were going across a dry streambed. Sure enough, when we reached the base of the mountain, rain began to fall, and the streambed began to fill with water. Getting back across it would not have been easy. The more the rain fell, the faster the stream became. Eventually, the stream was so active that we were now stuck on the other side of it. We had crossed our own Rubicon.

At work, you've probably had projects that involved making some difficult go or no-go decisions. At one company, I had a team of developers and we were going to create a new system to keep track of VHS video tapes, but we also knew that DVD was emerging. Should we make the system for VHS or for DVD? We only had enough resources to do one. After considering the matter, we opted to hope that DVD was going to catch-on and so we proceeded to focus on DVD's. We got lucky and it turned out to be one of the first such systems and even earned an award for its innovation. Crossed the Rubicon and luckily landed on the right side.

Of course, crossing the Rubicon can lead to bad results. Caesar was fortunate that he was not right away killed for his insubordination. Maybe his own troops might have even tried to kill him, since there were bound to be some that didn't want to get caught up in the whole you-are-condemned to death thing. The recent news story about the teenage soccer team in Thailand that went into the caves and became lost, and then the rain closed off their exit, it's something that they all easily could have died in those caves, were it not for the tremendous and lucky effort that ultimately saved them.

What does this all have to do with AI self-driving cars?

At the Cybernetic AI Self-Driving Car Institute, we are developing AI for self-driving cars. As we do so, there are often very serious and crucial "crossing the Rubicon" kinds of decisions to be made. These same decisions are being made right now by auto makers and tech firms also developing AI self-driving cars.

Let's take a look at some of those kinds of difficult and nearly undoable decisions that need to be made.

- LIDAR

LIDAR is a type of sensor that can be used for an AI self-driving car. It makes use of Light and Radar to help ascertain the world around the self-driving car. Beams of light are sent out from the sensor, the light bounces back like a radar wave, and the sensor is able to gauge the shapes of nearby objects by the length of time involved in the returns of the light waves. This can be a handy means to have the AI determine if there is a pedestrian that is standing ahead of the self-driving car and at a distance of say 15 feet. Or that there is a fire hydrant over to the right of the self-driving car at a distance of 20 feet. And so on.

AI self-driving cars tend to use conventional radar to try and identify the surroundings, they use sonic sensors to do likewise, and they use cameras to capture visual images and try to analyze what's around via vision related processing. They can also use LIDAR. There is no stated requirement that an AI self-driving car has to use any of those kinds of sensors. It is up to whatever the designers of the self-driving car decide to do.

That being said, it is hard to imagine that a self-driving car could properly operate in the real-world if you didn't have cameras on it and weren't doing vision processing of the images. You could maybe decide you'll only use cameras, but that's a potential drawback since there are going to be situations where vision alone won't provide a sufficient ability to sense the real-world around the self-driving car. Thus, you'd likely want to add at least radar. Now, with the cameras and radar, you have a fighting chance of being able to have a self-driving car that can operate in the real-world. Adding sonar would help further.

What about LIDAR? Well, if you only had LIDAR, you'd probably not have much of an operational self-driving car, so you'd likely want to add cameras too. Now, with LIDAR and cameras, you have a fighting chance. If you also add radar, you've further increased the abilities. Add sonic sensors and you've got even more going for you.

Indeed, you might say to yourself, hey, I want my self-driving car to have as many kinds of sensors that will increase the capabilities of the self-driving car to the maximum possible. Therefore, if you already had cameras, radar, and sonar, you'd likely be inclined to add LIDAR. That being said, you also need to be aware that nothing in life is free. If you add LIDAR, you are adding the costs associated with the LIDAR sensor. You are also increasing the nature of the AI programming required to be able to collect the LIDAR data and analyze it.

There are these major stages of processing for self-driving cars:
- Sensor data collection and interpretation
- Sensor fusion
- Virtual model updating
- AI action plan updating
- Car controls commands issuance

If you add LIDAR to the set of sensors for your self-driving car, you also presumably need to add the software needed to do the sensor data collection and interpretation of the LIDAR. You also presumably need to boost the sensor fusion to be able to handle trying to figure out how to reconcile the LIDAR results, the radar results, the camera vision processing results, and the sonar results. Some would say that makes sense because it's like reconciling your sense of smell, sense of sight, sense of touch, sense of hearing, and that if you lacked one of those senses you'd have a lesser ability to sense the world. You would likely argue that the overhead of doing the sensor fusion is worth what you'd gain.

Nearly all of the auto makers and tech firms would agree that LIDAR is essential to achieving a true AI self-driving car. A true AI self-driving car is considered by industry standards to be a self-driving car of a Level 5. There are levels less than 5 that are self-driving cars requiring a human driver. These involve co-sharing of the driving task with a human driver. For a Level 5 self-driving car, the idea is that the self-driving car is driven only by the AI, and there is no need for a human driver. The Level 5 self-driving car even is likely to omit entirely any driving controls for humans, and the Level 5 is expected to be able to drive the car as a human would (in terms of being able to handle any driving task to the same degree a human could do so).

It might then seem obvious that of course all self-driving cars would use LIDAR. Not so for Tesla. Tesla and Elon Musk have opted to go without LIDAR. One of Elon Musk's most famous quotes for those in the self-driving car field is this one:

"In my view, it's a crutch that will drive companies to a local maximum that they will find very hard to get out of. Perhaps I am wrong, and I will look like a fool. But I am quite certain that I am not."

Source: https://www.theverge.com/2018/2/7/16988628/elon-musk-lidar-self-driving-car-tesla

This is the crossing of the Rubicon for Tesla.

Right now and for the foreseeable future, they are not making use of LIDAR. It could be that they've made a good bet and everyone else will later on realize they've needlessly deployed LIDAR. Or, maybe there's more than one way to skin a cat, and it will turn out that Tesla was right about being able to forego LIDAR, while the other firms were right to not forego it. Perhaps both such approaches will achieve the same ends of getting us to a Level 5 self-driving car.

For Tesla, if they are betting wrong, it would imply that they will be unable to achieve a Level 5 self-driving car. And if that's the case, and the only way to get there is to add LIDAR, they would then need to add it to their self-driving cars. This would be a likely costly endeavor to retrofit and might or might not be viable. They might then opt to redesign future designs and write-off the prior models as unalterable, but at that point will be behind other auto makers, and will need to after-the-fact figure out how to integrate it into everything else. Either way, it's going to be costly and could cause significant delays and a falling behind of the rest of the marketplace.

It would also cause Tesla to have to eat crow, as it were, since they've all along advertised that your Tesla has "Full Self-Driving Hardware on All Cars" – which might even get them caught in lawsuits by Tesla owners that argue they were ripped-off and did not actually get all the hardware truly needed for a self-driving car. This could lead to class action lawsuits. It could drain the company of money and focus. It would likely cause the stock to drop like a rock.

This does not mean that Tesla couldn't re-cross the Rubicon and opt to add LIDAR, but it just shows that when you've made the decision to cross the Rubicon, going back is often somewhat infeasible or going to be darned hard to do.

I sometimes wonder if Elon Musk might have said "alea iacta est" when he made this rather monumental decision.

• Straight to Level 5

Another potential crossing of the Rubicon involves deciding whether to get to Level 5 by going straight to it, or instead to get there by progressing via Level 3 and Level 4 first.

Some believe that you need to crawl before you walk, and walk before your run, in order to progress in this world. For self-driving cars, this translates into achieving Level 3 self-driving cars first. Then, after maturing with Level 3, move into Level 4. After maturing with Level 4, move into Level 5. This is the proverbial "baby steps" at a time kind of approach.

Others assert that there's no need to do this progressively. You can skip past the intermediary levels. Just aim directly to get to Level 5. Some would say it is a waste of time to do the intermediary levels.

Others would claim you'll not get to Level 5 if you don't cut your teeth first on the lower levels. No one knows for sure.

Meanwhile, Waymo has pretty much made a bet that you can get straight to Level 5 and there's no need to do the intermediaries. They rather blatantly eschew the intermediary steps approach. They have taken the bold route of get to the moon or bust. No need to land elsewhere beforehand. Will they be right? Suppose their approach falls flat and it turns out those that got to Level 4 are able to make the leap to Level 5, meanwhile maybe the efforts underway on Level 5 aren't able to be finalized.

Does this mean that Waymo cannot re-cross the Rubicon and opt to first settle for a Level 4. As with all of these crossings, they could certainly back-down, though it would likely involve added effort, costs, and so on.

- Machine Learning Models

When developing the AI for self-driving cars, by-and-large it involves making use of various machine learning models. Tough choices are made about which kinds of neural networks to craft and what forms of learning algorithms to employ. Decisions, decisions, decisions.

Trying to later on change these decisions can be difficult and costly. It's another crossing of the Rubicon.

- Virtual World Model

At the crux of most AI self-driving car systems there is a virtual world model. It is used to bring together all of the information and interpretations about the world surrounding the self-driving car. It embodies the latest status gleaned from the sensors and the sensor fusion. It is used for the creation of AI action plans. It is crucial for doing what-if scenarios in real-time for the AI to try and anticipate what might happen next.

In that sense, it's like having to decide whether to use a Rubik's cube or use a Rubik's snake or a Rubik's domino. Each has its own merits. Whichever one you pick, everything else gets shaped around it. Thus, if you put at the core a virtual world model structure that is of shape Q, you are going to base the rest of the AI on that structure. It's no easy thing to then undo and suddenly shift to shape Z. It would be costly and involve gutting much of the AI system you'd already built.

It's once again a crossing of the Rubicon.

- Particular Brand/Model of Car

Another tough choice in some cases is which brand/model of car to use as the core car underlying your AI self-driving car. For the auto makers, they are of course going to choose their own brand/model. For the tech firms that are trying to make the AI of the self-driving car, the question arises as to whom do you get into bed with. The AI you craft will be to a certain extent particular to that particular car.

I know that some of you will object and say that the AI, if properly written, should be readily ported over to some other self-driving car. This is much harder than it seems. I assure you it's not just like re-compiling your code and voila it works on a different kind of car.

Furthermore, many of these tech firms are painting themselves into a corner. They are writing their AI code with magic numbers and other facets that will make porting the AI system nearly impossible. Without good commenting and thinking ahead about generalizing your system, it's going to be stuck on whatever brand/model you started with. The rush right now to get the stuff to work is more important than making it portable. There are many that will be shocked down the road that they suddenly realize they cannot overnight shift onto some other model car.

- Premature Roadway Release

This last example of crossing the Rubicon has to do with putting AI self-driving cars onto public roadways, perhaps doing so prematurely.

The auto makers and tech firms are eager to put their self-driving cars onto public roadways. It is a sign to the world that there is progress being made. It helps boost stock prices. It helps for the AI itself to gain "experience" from being driven miles upon miles. It helps the AI developers as they tune and fix the AI systems and do so based on real-world encounters by the self-driving car.

That's all well and good, except for the fact that it is a grand experiment upon the public. If the self-driving cars have problems and get into accidents, it's not going to be good times for self-driving cars. Indeed, it's the bad apple in the barrel in that even if only one specific brand of self-driving car gets into trouble, the public will perceive this as the entire barrel is bad.

If the public becomes disenchanted with AI self-driving cars, you can bet that regulators will change their tune and no longer be so supportive of self-driving cars. A backlash will most certainly occur. This could slow down AI self-driving car progress. It could somewhat curtail it, but it seems unlikely to stop it entirely. Right now, we're playing a game of dice and just hoping that few enough of the AI self-driving cars on the roadways have incidents that it won't become a nightmare for the whole industry.

This then is another example of crossing the Rubicon.

Putting AI self-driving cars onto the roadways, which if it turns out premature, might make it difficult to continue forward with self-driving cars, at least not at the pace that it is today.

For the AI self-driving car field, there are a plethora of crossings of the Rubicon. Some decision makers are crossing the Rubicon and doing so like Caesar, fully aware of the chances they are taking, and betting that in the end they've made the right choice. There are some decision makers that are blissfully unaware that they have crossed the Rubicon, and only once something untoward happens will they realize that oops, they made decisions earlier that now haunt them. Each of these decisions are not necessarily immutable and undoable per se, it's more like there is a cost and adverse impact if you've made the wrong choice and need to backtrack or redo what you've done.

I'd ask that all of you involved in AI self-driving cars make sure to be cognizant of the Rubicon's you've already crossed, and which ones are still up ahead. I'm hoping that by my raising your awareness, in the end you'll be able to recite the immortal words of Caesar: Veni, vidi, vici (which translates loosely into I came, and I saw, and I conquered).

CHAPTER 9
ADDICTED TO SELF-DRIVING CARS

CHAPTER 9

ADDICATED TO
SELF-DRIVING CARS

The United Nations has now declared officially that video gaming can be an addiction. Indeed, video gaming addiction will now be listed in the International Classification of Diseases by the World Health Organization (WHO).

It's been a long time coming, some say, and they are relieved that formal recognition of the addiction is now openly been declared. You might be an avid video game player that thinks this whole thing is a bunch of malarkey. You might be a video gamer that knows others that certainly seem addicted and now you know that you were possibly right. Or, you might be someone that says it's a lot of something about nothing – who cares whether it is classified as an addiction or not, you might say, and consider this meaningless and undue hullabaloo.

What's the story about video game addiction?

Well, for some players, it becomes an obsession that overtakes their lives. It admittedly is something that parents are more worried about than are the individuals themselves that are stricken by the addiction. There are parents that claim their video game addicted child or children have become anti-social and don't meet or speak face-to-face with their peers.

Parents say that their offspring have become sleep deprived and their day-to-day behavior has gotten sloppy and incoherent. They claim that their dearest is doing poorly in school and distracted from their academics by the non-stop playing time on the video games. Some parents even say that their child lacks vitamin D because they do not spend time in the sun anymore.

I realize that many teenagers scoff at all of this. They would say that they are actually very social oriented because they are playing multi-player games and interacting with others that are not just in the local city but are from around the world. These players would say that there's nothing unusual about having a hobby and wanting to pursue it. They try to remind their parents that just because they didn't have video games in their now bygone era, they did have other things like collecting stamps or building model ships, and why weren't their concerns then about stamp addiction or model ship building addiction.

Furthermore, for those video game players that lead otherwise relatively clean lives, they say that classifying video game playing as an addiction makes a mockery out of "real" addictions such as drugs. Imagine taking the police resources and health industry resources that should be dealing with drug addictions, and parceling off a piece of those resources to help corral video game addiction. For every hour spent on trying to help video game addicted people, it is a potentially one less hour that could have gone toward those that really suffer from an addiction that is bad for them and harmful to others around them (most studies would say that drug addiction leads to crime and other adverse consequences).

The counter argument is that video game addiction is silently undermining us. It is not as apparent and nor as visible as say drug addiction. It is insidious. It captures people, especially young people, and yet they don't realize it. If it then undercuts their education, if it undercuts their ability to interact face-to-face, we are gradually going to produce a next generation that will be incapable of running society and running themselves as adults. There is no barrier to entry per se, since you can just download a free game onto your smartphone and start playing. Getting illicit drugs takes more work and will be more readily detected and presumably stopped. Video game playing hooks you, and indeed many of today's video games are free because they are monetized by advertising.

What does it mean to have an addiction? This is a question being posed by some that think the video gaming addiction is incorrectly being classified as an addiction. Sure, video gaming can get out of hand, but to then say it is addictive, well, that seems like a wild leap of logic for some experts and everyday folks too. If my child plays for a few hours per day, does that constitute an addiction? Suppose they play on some days but not others. Suppose they are reading their textbooks and doing schoolwork, while simultaneously playing video games. Heck, there are some on-line textbooks that now include video gaming as part of the instructional delivery of the content – does that mean my child is addicted?

Generally, the WHO addiction classification involves these major elements:

- Severity of the addiction
- Impairment due to the addiction
- Prolonged nature of the addiction
- Stickiness of the addiction

In the case of severity, if the video game player has become all consumed by video gaming, it presumably is severe enough to be possibly an addiction. If it impairs what otherwise might be considered a normal life, it could be an addiction. This might be the adverse impact on schoolwork and also inhibiting of social skill development. If the video gamer has been doing this for weeks or months on end, it is prolonged and thus not something that just flirtingly happened (like say they did this for a week during summer camp). The stickiness is basically how hard is it to stop. An addiction is normally accompanied by great difficulty in kicking the habit.

These factors are all to be considered in combination. If someone is not fully engulfed by these factors together, it is less likely that it would be an addiction per se. It could still be bad for the person, but just not classified as an addiction. The addiction classification helps to bring the attention to the presumed malady and makes it more readily recognized and dealt with.

Some even liken these kinds of addictions to what are called a cultural impulse control disorder. As an aside, I know an avid professional video game player that has turned his pursuit into a professional career, and he wears a hoodie proudly emblazoned with "I Have a Cultural Impulse Control Disorder" and it shows a picture of one of his favorite video games. That's making light of something that others would say should be taken seriously. I suppose though that's the maverick imagery that video game players have of themselves, namely that they dare to be different, one might say.

What does this have to do with AI self-driving cars?

At the Cybernetic AI Self-Driving Car Institute, we are exploring ways in which humans might inadvertently become addicted to using AI self-driving cars. It's an interesting behavioral aspect worthy of consideration.

Conversations with Wilson

Have you ever seen the movie Castaway that has Tom Hanks in it? If you haven't seen the movie, don't read the rest of this paragraph since it is a movie spoiler. During the movie, he begins to anthropomorphize a volleyball, which he calls Wilson (of course, a branding opportunity). He seemingly believes that an inanimate object is a living person. He carries on conversations with Wilson, albeit a bit one-sided, and they are the best of buddies.

One concern for AI self-driving cars and the humans that will be occupying them are that some humans might begin to anthropomorphize the car. The AI will be interacting with the human occupants. A human rider begins to think they are speaking with a fellow human. Soon, the human becomes obsessed with their AI interaction. Eventually, it dovetails into an addiction. The human wants to speak to the AI and only the AI self-driving car. They withdraw from other humans. Etc.

If this seems overly farfetched, please be aware that some people have already started down this same kind of path with Siri and with Alexa. Also, there are cases of elderly that are homebound that begin to anthropomorphize their electronics in their home, such as a blood pressure machine that they use each day. It can happen. Now, that doesn't mean it will happen for AI self-driving cars, and nor that it can happen with any great frequency. But, keep in mind that presumably someday there will be AI self-driving cars all around us, just as today there are 200 million conventional cars. This implies that some percentage of the human population might become "addicted" to the AI of their AI self-driving car.

Another aspect about the potential addiction to self-driving cars involves the possibility of using an AI self-driving car around the clock. It is predicted that AI self-driving cars will be put to use 24×7. Even if you aren't using your own AI self-driving car, you might loan it to a friend or maybe use it for ridesharing to make a few extra bucks. You are presumably going to have your children use it, such as taking them to their dance practice or to their study group at school after-hours.

Some believe that there will be people that will essentially live in their AI self-driving car. You can sleep in it, and have it driving you to your far away work office or wherever else you want to go. You can work in it, presumably using the electronic communications to do a Skype or other kind of remote work activity. You can have it go thru a drive-thru to get you food. And so on.

Could this become a form of addiction? Some would say that it might be something done out of necessity. Rather than having a place to live, which maybe is costly for you, instead you pretty much live in your AI self-driving car. There might be special drive-up "car motels" wherein you are able to take a shower and use the facilities (like today's full-service truck stops), but otherwise you are living and sleeping in your AI self-driving car. There is a fine line between doing this for economic reasons, and doing it because you are addicted to the AI self-driving car. In any case, it might be a form of addiction, and have gone beyond just a necessity.

If a person opts to neglect walking, riding a bike, and eschews all other forms of transportation, and only and always insists of riding in their AI self-driving car, it could be a sign that perhaps an addiction is being formed. We need to consider as stated earlier the factors of addiction.

Here's the questions that would need to be asked about someone that might have an AI self-driving car addiction:

- What is the severity of their personal attachment to the AI self-driving car?
- Are they impaired in other aspects of their lives due to the attachment to the AI self-driving car?
- Is it a prolonged attachment or simply an intermittent one?
- Is it sticky in the sense that they seem to be unable to separate themselves away from their AI self-driving car?

Ridiculous, some would say. Crazy talk, others would argue. Nobody could fall into those behavioral traps, some assert.

When I present this somewhat novel idea at conferences, someone invariably says that there are automobile "fanatics" that love to care for their cars and know all about their cars. These people will spend endless hours tuning their car. They polish and shine their car night and day, wanting it to appear pristine. Are they suffering from an addiction? If we have people that do the same kind of thing with their AI self-driving car, are they ergo also "addicted" in the same manner (if you believe that this is a form of addiction)?

I come back to the factors involved when such a question arises. Possibly, it could be an addiction if the criteria of an addiction are satisfied by the nature of what the person does. Their behavior can exhibit addiction.

Let's suppose for the moment that someone could become addicted to their AI self-driving car (go with me on this, even if you think it a preposterous notion). What then? Well, for any addiction, usually there are attempts to treat the addiction. Are there ways for the person to find happiness in life other than via their addiction? Do they understand their addiction? Can they assist in the treatment? Addiction is considered a mental health issue.

Believe it or not, there are now video game player "addiction recovery centers" that will help break someone of their addiction to video games. You've probably heard of drug addiction recovery centers, well, there are now ones for video gamers too. Perhaps we might in the future have AI self-driving car "addiction recovery centers" that will do the same for those addicted to AI self-driving cars.

There are some that say that if we are willing to agree that video game playing can be an addiction, it's an easy step to then say that someone could be addicted to an AI self-driving car. Thus, no matter had nutty it might seem to suggest that we could have addiction to AI self-driving cars, you'd have to concede that if it can apply to video games then why not to an AI self-driving car.

Keen Interest in Video Games, Self-Driving Cars Correlated?

One audience member asked me if there might even be a correlation between someone that can get addicted to video games as to that same person being more readily addicted to AI self-driving cars. It's an intriguing question. We don't have enough AI self-driving cars on our roadways as yet to try and see if this can happen. Nonetheless, a keen interest in video games might somehow be related to having a keen interest in AI self-driving cars. That's a research study probably a few years from now.

Let's suppose then that you could become addicted to a self-driving car. Further, let's suppose that it gets classified by WHO as an official addiction. For treatment purposes, will health insurers pay to help that person get proper treatment? That's the same question being asked nowadays about video gamer addiction, but it's too soon yet to know what the health insurers are going to do about video gaming. Whatever they decide, it might then be applicable to AI self-driving car addiction.

What leads someone to become addicted? That's an ongoing argument that involves whether it is a kind of DNA biological predisposition or whether it is something learned. Maybe a person becomes addicted because it is in their blood. When they therefore have an opportunity to get addicted, they are predisposed towards it.

This is often said about for example smoking. Of course, there are ways too that the aspect itself helps to entrap the person. If the thing itself has built-in addictive properties, it can turn someone that maybe is already predisposed into falling into and readily becoming a full-fledged addict. This might be said of the tobacco in smoking, and it might be said in the case of video gaming that how the video game is designed can lead to addictive behavior (offering rewards and points, similar to a gambling addiction).

For video gaming addiction, some lawyers are now lining up to see if they can go after the video game makers for producing a potentially adverse health related product. These lawyers are emboldened by the official WHO classification of video gaming addiction. It will make arguing their case before a judge and jury a lot easier to accept. One might wonder, accordingly, whether if there ultimately is an addiction to AI self-driving cars, will lawyers go after the auto makers for having designed and built something that is addictive? Or, maybe go after the tech firms that developed the AI systems? Maybe.

I realize that the idea that an AI self-driving car could be addictive just seems outlandish right now. Keep in mind that there are so few AI self-driving cars today that we don't really yet know how their introduction will impact society. I am betting that if I asked you ten years ago whether a video game could be addictive, you'd likely have said no. You would have said that it could become a passion, but not an addiction. Ten years later, guess what, it's now an official addiction.

Please realize that I would not have even written this piece were it not for the WHO declaring that video gaming is an addiction. If out-of-the-blue I had voiced the notion that AI self-driving cars might become addictive, you'd have had no frame of reference for the idea.

It would have been easy to dismiss the idea entirely. But, now that we seem to agree that video gaming can be addictive, we should be looking towards other aspect of our increasingly electronically invaded lives to see if we might be in store for more of the same.

Just think, we might have an addicted video gamer that is playing their video games while inside and being addicted to their AI self-driving car. That's quite an overpowering kind of addiction.

CHAPTER 10
ULTRASONIC HARM AND SELF-DRIVING CARS

CHAPTER 10

ULTRASONIC HARM
AND
SELF-DRIVING CARS

The law of unintended consequences is going to impact AI self-driving cars. You can bet on it. Actually, as a society, we're likely mainly interested in the "adverse" unintended consequences side of that natural law, since there are bound to be lots of otherwise "favorable" unintended consequences – the favorable benefits we can all readily live with. It's the adverse ones that pose potential concern and could lead to harm.

You might recall that in the 1990's there was the advent of the passenger side airbags on cars, which everyone at first thought would be a great safety add-on to cars. Few cars had it initially and only the more expensive new cars were outfitted with it. Gradually, the cost dropped and most of the auto makers included those passenger side airbags in their basic models. So far, so good.

But, what began to emerge were reports of small children getting harmed when the passenger side airbags deployed. This was due to the aspect that small children and in particular babies in their special car seats were not the designated occupants that the airbag was intended to save. Those airbags were intended to save someone larger and older, such as teenagers and adults.

Unfortunately, it was actually at times harmful to the youngest occupants. It became recommended to put your baby in its car seat into the backseat of the car, thus avoiding getting harmed by a passenger side airbag that might deploy in an accident. This though led to parents forgetting that their baby was in the backseat of the car and produced hot-car deaths, another adverse unintended consequence.

The sad but telling point to the story is that something that was supposed to be good turned out to have unintended consequences. In this case, I've focused on the adverse unintended consequences. As a society, we need to determine whether the adverse unintended consequences are so bad that it perhaps causes us to rethink whether the innovation should be continued. Before an innovation is unleashed onto the world, presumably someone is calculating the risks versus rewards to ascertain that the ROI or rewards exceed the risks, but this is usually done only with respect to the intended consequences. Often, the unintended consequences are unforeseen. Once those unintended consequences are encountered, we need to rebalance the equation to include both the adverse unintended consequences and the favorable unintended consequences.

Thus, this:

- **Initial ROI calculation**: Risk versus rewards of Favorable intended consequences + Adverse intended consequences

- **Emergent ROI calculation**: Risk versus rewards of Favorable unintended consequences + Adverse unintended consequences

- **Full ROI calculation**: Risk versus rewards of Favorable intended consequences + Adverse intended consequences + Risk versus rewards of Favorable unintended consequences + Adverse unintended consequences

Let's take another example and see how it played out. In Australia, when they first mandated that bicycle riders must wear bike helmets, it was done to save lives. Research had shown that bike riders without helmets would often land on the ground at high speeds and their skulls would get damaged or cracked. Wearing a helmet seemed like a good idea. Rather than making it a voluntary act, the viewpoint was to make it mandatory. Of course, throughout the United States there are many jurisdictions that have done the same.

Pass a Helmet Law, Get Fewer Bike Riders

In this case of Australia, a follow-up study that was undertaken after the helmet law was first enacted discovered that many young people such as teenagers were no longer riding bikes at all, due to the helmet law. These young people perceived that wearing a helmet made them look bad, and culturally it was considered out-of-touch to wear the helmets. But they also faced strict enforcement of the helmet law and so they knew that if they rode their bikes and didn't wear the helmet they would likely get caught and punished. So, they opted to do less bike riding. The study suggested that this led to those young people doing much less exercise and tending toward becoming physically unfit or even overweight. This is another example of an adverse unintended consequence.

The rise of electronic devices in our lives has offered many great benefits, but they have also raised some adverse consequences. Remember the argument that holding a cell phone to your ear could possibly cause cancer? This is still being debated today. Another adverse aspect involves possibly playing games on your smartphone and doing so to the extent that you become anti-social and no longer communicate human-to-human with those around you. These adverse aspects are considered unintended consequences. In theory, nobody that designed and is selling these phones is doing so to purposely make people become anti-social and nor so that they will get cancer.

Another example of the potential dangers of electronic devices might be the underlying explanation for the sicknesses that have befallen the United States diplomats that were stationed in Cuba and that were stationed in China. You might have seen in the news that there were U.S. diplomats in both of those countries that began to say that they were experiencing an unusually large number of headaches and dizziness. At times, it was a mild aspect. For some of those diplomats it became debilitating. The symptoms seem to come and go, for some of the diplomats, while others of those complaining about the health concerns appear to have more enduring complications, and deeper complications such as ongoing nausea and other incapacitating problems.

No one really knows what is causing the health issues. Could it be mass hysteria that has overtaken them? This seems highly unlikely. Could it be something they ingested like water or food? This also has been generally ruled out. Could it be some kind of deliberate attack against them? This certainly seems like a strong possibility because of who they are and what they represent, thus, it is a carved out slice of the population that have in common their work mission. But, Cuba and China have indicated that this is nothing they have caused and do not know what is producing these results.

One of the latest theories is that it might be something electronically based. Maybe these diplomats are being targeted with some kind of special ray gun. The ray gun beams electro-magnetic waves at them. The intensity and prolonged nature of exposure to the rays then causes the symptoms that have been reported. It could be some new sneaky approach to "invisible" attacks against our diplomats. The U.S. State Department is investigating these matters and not yet stated whether these are deliberate attacks and nor whether there is any kind of electronic connection to the matter.

Another similar theory is that the symptoms are indeed electronically based but perhaps accidental in their consequences. Perhaps the diplomats have been working or living in a building that so happens to have an abundance of electronic sensory devices and that the ultrasonic signals that emanate from those devices are the culprit to all of this. The motion detectors surrounding them, the air-quality sensors, the automatic light switches, and so on, perhaps those in-combination are producing a bombardment of signals that fall outside our hearing range, and yet can also impact our brains.

The prolonged exposure to these ultrasonic signals might be scrambling the neurons of the human brain and thus leading to the dizziness and headaches. Consequent symptoms like the nausea and the rest might all be attributed to the distortions to the brain. If the distortions are long lasting, it could lead to a long lasting physical manifestation of the symptoms in the rest of the human body. High frequency noise has been shown to have adverse consequences that can produce these kinds of health issues.

If you are the suspicious type of person, you might even suspect that the governments in those locations have maybe opted to purposely cause this. Perhaps they are using special ray guns that produce ultrasonic signals and they are beaming them at our diplomats. Why? Maybe to see whether it works to harm and disrupt them, and maybe as an experiment to ascertain whether it might be handy for other situations and against other potential "enemies" when needed.

If you are a less suspicious person, you might go with the explanation that maybe there was some kind of experiment, and maybe it wasn't quite so lethal, but that it combined with other ultrasonic "exhaust" already in that location. Thus, let's suppose there is a normal amount of ultrasonic exhaust, and you add to it with a bit more for the "experiment" and then the combined total goes over a threshold. In that sense, the experiment wasn't purposely trying to harm, and maybe it was a listening device that was supposed to be able to listen-in on our diplomats. This is seemingly less evil in that they were indeed doing something untoward, but not in a means that was quite so dastardly.

Nobody knows right now for sure. Well, at least nobody is openly telling what it is. Could be a secretive cold war kind of fight taking place and maybe the public will never know what happened. The main "solution" right now has been to remove the diplomats from where they are working and living, and hopefully wait and see that the symptoms subside. Let's hope that however it has occurred that there isn't any permanent damage to them.

With the advent of ultrasonic tones throughout our daily lives, maybe all of us are gradually getting similar exposure. There are devices such as automatic door openers and smart street lights that tend to give off some amount of ultrasonic exhaust. We might all be daily exposed to these same kinds of signals. You might not be getting sufficient exposure to yet react to it. Or, you might react to it and shrug it off as some other aspect, like maybe you aren't getting enough sleep or maybe that you bumped your head on a low doorway frame the other day.

What does this have to do with AI self-driving cars?

At the Cybernetic AI Self-Driving Car Institute, we are examining whether the use of numerous sensory devices on a self-driving car might have unintended adverse consequences due to ultrasonic exhaust.

Let's consider this aspect for a moment. The good news about AI self-driving cars is that they potentially can save lives and make our world into a better place. Those are some of the stated intended consequences. True self-driving cars, considered at the Level 5, will drive entirely without human intervention, and indeed the thinking is that a human driver won't be allowed – no driving controls for a human, and instead it is entirely and exclusively driven by the AI. Some say that this means that ultimately humans won't be allowed to drive at all, and for those that like driving a car, this seems like an adverse intended consequence.

What about potential unintended consequences?

Potential Unintended Consequence of Ultrasonic Exhaust

One such potential unintended consequence of self-driving cars might be that we would become exposed to ultrasonic exhaust.

I am sure we would all agree that we can classify this as an adverse unintended consequence, rather than being considered a favorable one (unless you have an evil plot to destroy mankind and figure this is a means maybe to do so; or maybe try to beam some kind of mind control at humans as they go around in their AI self-driving cars!). There really is not much dispute that there will be some amount of ultrasonic exhaust, which comes with the territory of the sensory devices on an AI self-driving car. The question arises as to how much is too much?

There's an added twist too. One key idea is that a confluence of ultrasonic rays is the manner in which this happens, namely that if you have a lot of devices doing the ultrasonic exhaust, they in accumulation lead to excessive amounts that are then harmful. Not just one everyday electronic device is likely to be enough exposure. Well, we know that an AI self-driving car is a smorgasbord of electronic devices. You've got your radar devices, back and front of the self-driving car. You've got your sonar devices all around the self-driving car. You've got a LIDAR device on the self-driving car, depending upon the type of self-driving car. And so on.

Therefore, by design, a self-driving car is chock full of electronic devices. This means that the opportunity for them to create a confluence is pretty high. When the self-driving car is in motion, you can bet that nearly all of those electronic sensory devices will be active. Indeed, at higher speeds they are even more active in order to detect what's going on around the self-driving car. As it were, as a human occupant in a self-driving car, you will be in a virtual shower of ultrasonic exhaust. It will be all around you, and you won't see it.

Sometimes we can hear the ultrasonic exhaust. It depends on the nature of your hearing and the nature of the frequencies of the ultrasonic sounds. It has been reported that some of the diplomats claim they believe they did hear tones in their ears, or sometimes a tingling sensation in their ears. Was this real? Or, is it something in hindsight that they believe because they are told that it might be an ultrasonic bombardment? Even if they did hear something, perhaps it has nothing to do with the situation at hand at all. Again, still a mystery.

In addition to the sensory devices on the self-driving car, you are likely to have something like Siri or Alexa on-board too. The odds are that you'll talk to and with your AI self-driving car. Take me to the ballgame, you tell your AI self-driving car. Stop at the market so I can get some beer on the way, you command. A few years ago this idea of talking to your car might have seemed space age and science fiction like. Given the popularity nowadays of speech interaction systems via our smartphones and specialized devices, I think we can all agree that it is highly likely that these speech interacting systems will be used in AI self-driving cars, and there's nothing odd or peculiar or unusual about it.

This though means more ultrasonic sounds will be involved. Yet again adding to the confluence. Furthermore, there is a potential added "adverse unintended consequence" to the use of the in-car commands capabilities, namely that someone nefarious can try to send sound signals to your in-car command system and take over the control of your self-driving car. There have been experiments shown that via high-frequency ultrasonic sounds that aren't heard by humans, you can send commands to Siri and Alexa, and those systems will act on those commands as though they were spoken directly to those devices. This is a loophole that hopefully will ultimately be closed off.

What else have we got inside the electronic bazaar of an AI self-driving car? Well, you've got your full-on entertainment system. Since we will be in our AI self-driving cars a lot, maybe around the clock, you might have big screen TV's inside your self-driving car. You might have some kind of LED external displays on the outside of your self-driving car, doing advertising and generating you some cash by the advertisers eager to use your self-driving car to push their wares. More and more ultrasonic signals that can be added to the confluence.

Suppose you opt to essentially live in your AI self-driving car. You go to work in it. You sleep at night in it, perhaps while it is driving you to your next destination or wherever. You use it for trips to the store. You use it for going to a vacation spot. All the time, maybe getting exposed to ultrasonic exhaust. Today, most people are only in their cars for short bursts of time. In the future, it is likely you'll be spending extended periods of time in your AI self-driving cars.

What about your children that will be extensively using your family AI self-driving car? They'll get exposed too to the ultrasonic exhaust. What about other human occupants, such as if you opt to turn your AI self-driving car into a ridesharing vehicle. You rent it out for use, hoping to make some money and cover the cost and expenses of the AI self-driving car. Perhaps each of those occupants also now becomes exposed to the ultrasonic exhaust.

Who will be responsible if we later on discover that the amount of ultrasonic exhaust was harmful? You, the owner of the AI self-driving car? Or, the auto maker that made the car? Or, the tech firm that did the electronics and the AI of the self-driving car? It could be a messy legal matter to sort out. Worse, still, the health harm could have arisen, occurring before we even knew that it could happen, and ended-up harming a lot of people.

That's a potential adverse unintended consequence, for sure.

Should we just wait and see how this plays out?

Hopefully, instead, we'll all be working toward figuring it out beforehand. It really should be in the category of potential "intended" adverse consequences, rather than the unintended bucket. We are already aware of the possibility, so let's get to it now. How much ultrasonic exhaust are we as a society willing to allow, given that the AI self-driving car has so many other societal benefits. There's that risk versus reward equation to be dealt with.

I'd even wager that there is an additional exposure that goes beyond just your own individual AI self-driving car. Once we have lots of AI self-driving cars on our roadways, will this then allow for even greater levels of confluence. There you are, heading along on the freeway, in your AI self-driving car, and not a care in the world. Meanwhile, next to your car there is another AI self-driving car – in fact, you have other AI self-driving cars to your left, to your right, in front of you, and behind you. Suppose the ultrasonic exhaust spills over into your AI self-driving car?

It could be that maybe a solo AI self-driving car only produces some amount N of ultrasonic exhaust, not enough to directly harm you, but when the surrounding AI self-driving cars are producing some amount Y, the combined N plus Y is sufficient to harm those nearby.

Thus, even if you study the impact of one AI self-driving car, you might be missing the bigger picture that someday they will be all around us. The confluence might only be triggered once there are enough of them on the roadways and driving relatively near to each other.

One possibility of resolving this consists of lowering the amount of ultrasonic exhaust being emitted. This requires likely redesigning the electronic devices that are being used on AI self-driving cars. No one is going to worry about a costly redesign until or if someone says that there are dangers from the ultrasonic exhaust.

Another possibility consists of some form of shielding within the AI self-driving car or something that surrounds the sensory devices to dampen the ultrasonic exhaust. This though again requires a belief that there is a potential harm and so worth the cost to devise. It also could increase the weight and size of the devices, all of which will impact the weight and size of the AI self-driving car. It might rise the costs of the AI self-driving car, making it less affordable. It might turn it into a heavy tank, impacting gas mileage or EV consumption, and so on.

We need to keep at top-of-mind that for each such solution there is a likely intended and unintended consequence.

Allow me to offer the added thought that we don't yet know that this ultrasonic exhaust is even an issue at all. Some might contend that we don't have any proof as yet that the ultrasonic exhaust was the culprit in the case of the Cuba and China incidents. Nor do we have any proof that an AI self-driving car might have this kind of unintended adverse consequence. I agree that it's speculation and conjecture at this time.

It's timely for the AI self-driving car industry to consider doing experiments and research to try and ascertain whether there is any validity to these potential concerns. A colleague the other day said to me that he was going to put a bunch of white mice into a self-driving car and have it drive them around for a week to see what happens. I realize the idea of the ultrasonic exhaust might elicit these kinds of comments (he wasn't serious; it was his way of making a joke about it).

I'm not so sure that we should just laugh off the matter. I don't want to be accused of falsely saying that the sky is falling, and so don't please mistake my remarks in that manner. Just figured that I'd bring up something worthy of consideration. And, try to get us to consider it beforehand, rather than after-the-fact when the damage has already been done.

CHAPTER 11

ACCIDENTS CONTAGION

AND

SELF-DRIVING CARS

CHAPTER 11

ACCIDENTS CONTAGION AND SELF-DRIVING CARS

A contagion is usually considered a virus that spreads from person to person. Contagion can also generally be used to mean that some kind of practice or idea is spread, usually one of a harmful nature.

At a recent presentation that I gave about AI self-driving cars, I was asked whether there is a kind of "accidents contagion" occurring with the current crop of driverless self-driving cars. The question seemed to be based on the aspect that there appears to have been a recent spate of self-driving car related accidents. Is this perhaps a trend? Does it portend that the self-driving cars are an evil that is being unwisely spread? Should society try to take some kind of action to prevent further spread?

Let's now take a look at what's happening with these self-driving car accidents. Most notably, in the last few months we've had these:

- March 2018: Uber Volvo XC90 runs over and kills a pedestrian
- March 2018: Tesla Model X crashes into median and kills human driver
- May 2018: Waymo Chrysler Pacifica minivan gets into car accident with minor injuries

Each of those made big headlines. Instantly, there were some that were wringing their hands and saying that this is the end of AI self-driving cars. Some suggest that we were promised perfection in that the advent of self-driving cars would mean that there would no longer be any deaths or injuries associated with being in a car.

I'd like to clear up some of these misconceptions and myths. I'll use these recent incidents to illuminate some important aspects about AI self-driving cars.

At the Cybernetic AI Self-Driving Car Institute, we are developing AI systems for self-driving cars, and try to help business and society have a more balanced understanding of what such systems can do today and what they hopefully will be able to do in the future.

Reality About Self-Driving Cars on Our Roads

For those that believe we are going to have no more injuries or deaths while on our roadways, I would say that your only hope right now would be to ban car travel entirely, regardless whether using a conventional car or a self-driving car. Inevitably, no matter what foreseeably happens in the near future, there are going to be injuries and deaths involving conventional cars and also with AI self-driving cars.

Some say that once we have only and exclusively AI self-driving cars on the roadways that we'll no longer have any car related injuries or deaths. This seems like an unlikely premise. If a pedestrian suddenly steps in front of an AI self-driving car, unless that self-driving car has wings and can fly, it's going to hit that pedestrian if the physics don't allow any other option. A self-driving car is still a car. It cannot suddenly disobey the laws of physics. Also, self-driving cars are going to have mechanical problems and breakdowns, just like conventional cars.

We also need to consider the practicality of the idea that we would have only AI self-driving cars on our roadways. Right now, we have about 200 million conventional cars in the United States alone. They are not going to magically disappear or be transformed into AI self-driving cars overnight. Society has yet to decide whether or not this notion of not allowing conventional cars is even something we can all agree to have happen. In essence, for a very long time, we're going to have human driven cars intermixing with AI self-driving cars.

As such, you can toss whatever you want to into the AI self-driving car side of things, including the potential for V2V (vehicle-to-vehicle communications) and V2I (vehicle-to-infrastructure) communications, but nonetheless with the mixing of human driven cars and self-driving cars there are going to be collisions. A human driver can cause it by ramming into an AI self-driving car, or even an AI self-driving car could "cause" it by somehow not detecting a human driven car or failing to properly predict the actions of an AI self-driving car.

News Media Loves a Good/Bad Story

There is an ongoing love-hate relationship of the news media with AI self-driving cars. One minute, the major media outlets are touting that AI self-driving cars will save mankind. Society will be utterly transformed. It's as though the adoption of AI self-driving cars will cure cancer and solve world hunger, all at the same time.

Admittedly, the AI self-driving car adoption will eventually and gradually transform our society, including potentially allowing mobility unlike what we've seen before. Indeed, many predict that we are heading towards a new kind of economy called the "passenger economy." I'd like to rein in the expectations about how far the AI self-driving car though will solve other of society ills. Climate change? Homelessness? Crime? It's a bit of a reach to start claiming that we'll all be better off per se in those other areas.

As an aside, I'll add a bit of a twist. I claim that if we can really craft true AI Level 5 self-driving cars, which can drive a car in whatever a manner a human can, and if that means that we have then achieved some truer sense of AI, we might then have a chance at other major societal ramifications. In other words, AI that is that advanced and so adept, could be put to many other uses in society, presumably, beyond just being able to drive a car. There are some that say that we can achieve true Level 5 without AI becoming so good that it is more like true AI, and in which case the AI won't lend itself to other domains. We'll need to see how this plays out.

Okay, so we've now covered the love part of the love-hate relationship with the news media. The hate part also comes to play. Build them up, and knock them down, it's a popular refrain for anyone wanting to try and get views or readership. Whenever an AI self-driving car stumbles, it's going to get some pretty prominent attention. It becomes a man-bites-dog kind of story. We were just getting used to the idea that AI self-driving cars will solve our world problems, and then, bang, an AI self-driving car does something bad. Knocks the air right out of the balloon.

In the end, the magnification becomes perhaps overly confusing. Are these isolated cases or something more endemic? The major media usually doesn't take the time to consider these matters. Get the headline going and get some attention. A few minutes later, something else will be of keener interest.

In my list of the three recent incidents, Waymo is likely exasperated that they are being lumped together with the other two incidents. The Waymo occurrence only involved minor injuries, while the other two incidents involved deaths. Is it fair or reasonable to lump together incidents that are relatively minor with those that have the ultimate consequence? The overarching theme seems to usually be that these are self-driving cars, they are backed by big auto makers and tech firms, and they have gotten into trouble of one kind or another.

Statistical Chances Continue To Increase

Some people ask me why these occurrences "suddenly" seem to be increasing? Suppose I ask you stand in a batting cage. I will start tossing baseballs at you. Consider the pace and frequency involved. You duck and move, and generally can avoid getting hit. I then ask five friends to join me in tossing baseballs at you. Ouch, things are getting rough. I next add five more friends. At this point, you can barely avoid getting hit by the baseballs.

In the case of AI self-driving cars, we are gradually and inexorably having more and more of them on our roadways. If we assume that there is some kind of statistical chance per each AI self-driving car that it will ultimately get into a car accident, we are increasing our chances by the sheer volume involved. This is not the only factor. We also have that by-and-large the early adopters of self-driving cars were more likely to be mindful of learning what their self-driving car can and cannot do. Once we start toward the masses, you're going to have more and more owners that aren't going to be so careful.

We also have the factor that at first the other human driven cars were being cautious when coming upon an AI self-driving car. You could readily recognize such a car by the cone head that housed the LIDAR. Gradually, it is becoming harder to discern what is a self-driving car and what is not. Furthermore, even if you can detect that it is a self-driving car, you might not care in the sense that you won't change how you drive. No more Mr. Nice Guy, and instead it's all drivers for themselves, human or AI.

The formula is simple. Add more AI self-driving cars to our streets. Increase the number of miles being driven. Add humans that aren't as careful as maybe they once were. Spice this with potentially untested portions of AI self-driving cars that are now revealed while on our roads. You've got yourself more accidents.

Confusion About the Levels of Self-Driving Cars

Not all AI self-driving cars are the same. I say this because I often see people and the media blurring the aspect that there are true Level 5 self-driving cars, and then anything less than a Level 5 is considered a self-driving car that requires a human driver. The human driver is considered responsible for the self-driving car at less than a Level 5.

If there is an accident involving a less than Level 5 self-driving car, should we consider that to be on par with an accident involving a Level 5 self-driving car? Most would say that you can't compare the two. It's like apples versus oranges. In the less than Level 5, there is a co-shared responsibility with a human and so somehow the incident might have occurred because of the human failing, and thus we should not point fingers at the AI.

There are those that take this to the extreme and suggest that no matter what happens with a less then Level 5 self-driving car, it is the fault of the human. The human is the captain of that ship. No matter what else happens to the ship, it's the captain at fault. This seems like a stretch. If the AI suddenly hands over controls of the self-driving car, and there's one second left to go, and the self-driving car is heading into a wall, can we really reasonably say that this calamity is due to the human driver? Was the human driver supposed to somehow know that the AI self-driving car was going to ram the car into the wall?

Marketing and Advertising to Promote Self-Driving Cars

The auto makers and tech firms are putting millions upon millions of dollars into the self-driving car approach. Naturally, they want to market and advertise these advances. There is a fierce sense of competitiveness in the auto industry and each auto maker tries to outdo the other. Consumers can be fickle. If they perceive that a particular brand or model has something they think they want, those fickle consumers are willing to jump ship to some other car line. No more of the days wherein you stayed with the same auto maker that your parents used.

What's even more beguiling for some auto makers and tech firms is that often the consumer doesn't even know what features the car actually has. And, if they do, sometimes the consumer doesn't actively use the features. Instead, it's more akin to having bragging rights. My car can parallel park itself. How many times have you used this feature? Not yet. How long have you had the car? Two years. Sigh. Imagine that you were the engineers and AI developers that created the capability, you tested it, you fielded it, and the auto maker advertised and marketed it. All so that it would sit silently and never be used.

Public perception is being shaped by the marketing and advertising that is gradually growing and becoming bolder about the self-driving car capabilities. At some point, it could be that the suggested claims or implications of the ads and marketing might go over-the-line and become misleading and deceptive. Accusations such as this are emerging by various consumer watchdog groups already.

There is certainly a danger that the blitzkrieg of messages about AI self-driving cars might cause people to falsely believe that self-driving cars and AI has some kind of super powers. In that sense, having the media to bring potentially the marketplace back to reality is going to be helpful. Bombardment by paid-for radio ads, TV ads, billboards, and print ads about how incredibly safe AI self-driving cars is, does need to be tempered by the news media providing the other side of that coin.

Testing, Testing, Testing

When I discuss AI self-driving cars with those that aren't in-depth on the topic, they are often shocked to discover that the AI self-driving cars on our roads today are pretty much a large societal experiment. We have all collectively allowed our roadways to be used for testing. That self-driving car next to you has not been utterly verified to be completely error-free. I know that I'll get howls from fellow AI developers that will argue that you can never have a provable error-free AI self-driving car. Indeed, they point out that if that's what society demands, you might as well put all of the self-driving cars into mothballs and forget about getting to self-driving cars for now.

The argument about never being able to mathematically prove the safety and assurance of an AI self-driving car is somewhat of a red herring. I will absolutely concede that the world is not aiming to require the auto makers and tech firms to provide a full and proper proof of correctness. This though doesn't mean that then you can just let anything you want to end-up on our public roadways. There needs to be some diligence and sufficient amount of testing beforehand to reasonably know what might happen on our public roadways.

And the other aspect is the danger that somewhere within these complex AI systems there are lurking bugs. They are in there. It's more a question of how severe the bugs are. Plus, you need to consider what the rest of the AI system will do when a bug is encountered. An AI self-driving car that is barreling along at 70 miles per hour on the freeway, and if there's a hidden bug that when encountered causes the AI to try and issue an untoward command to the car controls, well, this is the kind of thing that requires the software to have double-checks and triple checks. It is though difficult to layer too many checks into the system because it is also faced with having to act and react in real-time. The more safety checks you pile-on, it could be that in the act of trying to prevent a problem you've caused another problem because the AI fails to take needed action on a timely basis.

Conclusion

Is the sky falling?

Are we seeing an "accidents contagion" that will continue to widen and spread?

I don't think the sky is falling, but I do think we ought to be looking upward at the sky and realize that there is rain coming and possibly a storm. I say this because the general public might gradually become overtly concerned about the safety of AI self-driving cars, which will then drive the regulators to also step in more so. To-date, the regulators have allowed a lot of latitude via mild regulations in an effort to avoid stifling what seems to be a grand innovation and that will brighten the future.

There isn't per se an accidents contagion in that there's nothing that is spreading these accidents from one self-driving car to another. There's not a hacker virus or something like that. We might someday see something along those lines, and so computer security needs to be at the top of the list for the auto makers and tech firms developing AI self-driving cars, but right now that's not a pressing issue as yet. The accidents aren't tied to another in any kind of daisy chain. Each is essentially independent of the other.

But, that's not to say that they aren't all based on the same core. All the auto makers and tech firms are generally taking the same overall approach to designing, coding, testing, and fielding their AI self-driving cars. In that sense, they all will generally suffer the same limitations and experience the same kinds of accidents. Plus, they are all mixing into the same general environment, doing so by putting these self-driving cars into the mix with human driven cars.

For self-driving car accidents, if you are an auto maker or tech firm and you want to minimize the chances of an accident, you would only allow your self-driving cars to be operated in a geographical area that you knew would be least likely to produce accidents. Would you put your self-driving car into the middle of New York City, where the crazy traffic is something that even the best human drivers dread, or would you put your self-driving car into Smalltown, USA where the streets are calm and the traffic is easy going. The problem though with putting all your eggs into the quiet town is that you won't then really know whether your self-driving car and its AI can scale-up to handle the downtown wild driving.

Some auto makers and tech firms have considered whether it might be best to keep their self-driving cars a bit under wraps and let others take a higher risk of having accidents, and those risk takers gaining the ire of the public, and having their brand tarnished. Meanwhile, the other auto makers or tech firms figure that after those others have taken those first-mover blows, it then clears the landscape for them to then introduce their self-driving cars and say that theirs is the new-and-improved version.

The usual tech firm bravado is one that says get there first and take the market before anyone else can, leaving just the crumbs for those that come along later on. The nature of AI self-driving cars though might not lend itself to the same kind of fail-fast, fail-first attitude of Silicon Valley, and the backlash could hurt those innovators. Worse still, it could cause the tide to recede for all. As the old line goes, all boats rise with the rising tide, but the boats also all drop lower with the receding tide.

CHAPTER 12
NON-STOP 24X7
AND
SELF-DRIVING CARS

CHAPTER 12

NON-STOP 24X7
AND SELF-DRIVING CARS

How often do you use your car?

I am betting you likely use your car in the morning to drive to work, and it then sits there, parked, until you drive home after work. For much of the time, you aren't actively using your car and instead it sits, waiting at your beck and call, and like a faithful steed is ready to go whenever you are (well, assuming it starts, and that it is well maintained). When you think about this, you might realize that you've purchased an asset that most of the time is unused. It's a resource that remains idle most of the day and night. It also loses value over time, decaying or otherwise aging, and becomes less usable and costlier to maintain.

Given that there are about 200 million cars in the United States alone, one could make the argument that we are a seemingly selfish society in that we each assume or demand that we need to possess our own car, which uses up the collective riches of the society, and yet this costly resource is only utilized a fraction of the available time. For most people, their car is their next costliest purchase, second to the purchase of a house. Thus, this is a big economic aspect and it's not like we are talking about having your shoes idle for a lot of the time that they could be used. Cars are expensive. It's a big deal.

Estimates are that our cars are parked 95% of the available time that they could be used (using 24×7 as the "available time" metric). This staggering 95% means that we are only using our cars about 5%

of the available time.

You might argue with me and assert that you wouldn't be using your car when you are asleep, so for me to suggest that your car could be used 24 hours per day is maybe unfair. Okay, let's subtract 8 hours out of a 24-hour day and say that we'll grant that cars won't be used while the owner is asleep (we'll revisit this assumption later on). In that case, cars are not being used an estimated 92.5% of the time versus 95%, and thus being used only about 7.5% of the time (this is based on surveys that suggest we use our cars for 1.2 hours per day, and so for a 24-8 =16 hour day it would be 1.2/16 = 7.5%).

Multiply this by 200 million cars and you have a staggering sense of the magnitude of the resource that is idle most of the time. Is this a misuse of these resources? Are we denying ourselves a greater economic value for the steep investment we put into these resources? There appears to be untapped value that we could leverage to the benefit of us all, both collectively and on an individual basis.

How can we solve this problem? Generally, the biggest constraint that holds back the more effective use of the resource is one thing, the driver.

A car does you little good if there isn't a driver. Without a driver, it's a parked car. It's a paperweight. Sure, you can store your stuff in it, and you can even use it as an in-car delivery mechanism. You can stare at it. You can admire it. You can show it off to your friends. But, other than serving in this limited ornamental fashion, it has little it can do when there isn't a driver.

Now that I've stated the problem in those terms, we can begin to find ways to solve it. If the constraint is the lack of a driver, perhaps we need to make available more drivers, or find more drivers that could use the resource. This though creates other problems. If I let my friend, Joe, use my car when I am not using it, will my car be available when I really need it? The great thing about owning a car is that you can usually have it at your beck and call. Once you've parked it, you know it will be there, unless maybe you are illegally parked and it gets towed away.

We want then to retain the benefit of the car being immediately available, when needed, if needed, and control its individual availability. At the same time, we need a driver in order to make it more effective as a resource. Just posting on Facebook that my car is available after I get home from work and until I need it in the morning, and offering it to anyone else, well, yes, there are specialized sites that provide this social networking, but it's a pretty small amount of people that do this.

As mentioned too, if I let another driver have my car, there's not much I can do to make sure that they will bring back my car the moment I need it (suppose I wake-up at 2 a.m. and just absolutely need to drive over to a burger place and get myself a late night snack, while Joe has driven my car to the other side of town for bar hopping).

Imagine if you could have a driver always available. A willing chauffeur that sits in your car, at all times, and can be invoked by you, as needed, when needed. Could you hire someone to be this chauffer? You could, but it would likely be costly (you'd need to pay them, and maybe cover their expenses, and if it is just one person they might not like sitting in your car for 24 hours per day, each day, waiting to drive you – those pesky humans!). Let's instead shift our focus from a human chauffer to instead using automation that acts like a chauffeur.

Would you still use your car for only 5% of the time that it could be used?

There are some people that might not change how they use their car. They might use their car in exactly the same way they do today. On the other hand, wouldn't it be tempting while at work to have your car go get you some lunch, so that you could just come down from your office and meet up with your car in the parking lot, and it already went over to get you pizza. Or, maybe your kids need to be picked-up from school, and instead of having to rush your guts to get to them, you calmly send your car to pick them up and then take them home, and then the car comes back to your workplace.

That's the promise of AI self-driving cars.

To clarify, that's the promise of true AI self-driving cars. A true self-driving car is considered a Level 5, which is a self-driving car that can drive in whatever manner a human can drive a car, and for which there is no human intervention needed to drive the car. For cars at a level less than a 5, a human driver is still needed in the car. Therefore, when referring herein to a self-driving car that has its own internal chauffeur, please keep in mind that I'm alluding to just the Level 5 true self-driving cars.

If you read the major news outlets coverage of self-driving cars, you might think that just any kind of self-driving car is going to get us to this potential non-stop 24×7 capability. Not really. It's the true Level 5 self-driving cars that will do so.

Furthermore, the major news outlets tend to gush at the idea that our cars can be used 24×7. Yes, it definitely will allow us to better maximize this expensive resource. It will tap into that untapped value. The benefits for society are impressive.

Wear and Tear on 24×7 Self-Driving Car a New Challenge

One question that does not seem to be getting any attention involves the aspect of whether our cars can cope with being run non-stop 24×7.

Think about the amount of wear and tear that your car gets today. Whatever amount it gets, this is based on 5% of usage. Will that car be able to cope with adding an additional 95% of the usage time? How long will your tires last? How long will it be before you need to change oil on the car? How long will it be before some of the engine parts break down? And so on.

Our present day cars are not made to work in this kind of non-stop 24×7 mode. You might assume that they can, but this has not yet been tried on a massive scale. Suppose we switch over to all AI self-driving cars, somehow, magically, and thus we take the 200 million conventional cars that are now being used only 5% of the time, and we wave a magic wand and we now have 200 million AI self-driving cars that are running all day and night, day after day, for 100% of the time.

Yikes, I'd bet that we're going to have those AI self-driving cars visiting the maintenance shop, very frequently.

You would also assume that the degree of breakdowns is probably going to increase. In other words, if today you only have your carburetor go out every so many years, it's going to happen every so many weeks or months instead, and possibly cause other parts to also wear out or break. You can't just assume that the car failures of today will simply be more frequent, and you likely need to consider that they will be more frequent and of a greater depth and degree.

Today's cars are not designed and built with the expectation they will run non-stop 24×7. We don't even really know how cars will react to this kind of bruising usage. Car parts aren't built to take this kind of punishment. We must then consider that either we accept the idea that our AI self-driving cars are going to have lots of physical failures and failings, simply due to the extended use, or we need to have the auto makers take another look at the makings of a car and figure out if somehow cars need to be redesigned and differently manufactured to cope with the non-stop 24×7.

If we end-up having to completely redesign the physical aspects of a car, in order to accommodate the desired non-stop 24×7, the odds are that the cost of an AI self-driving car is going to go up. Rather than simply using a conventional car that has the added AI self-driving car elements, we might need entirely new cars, ones that are built from the ground up to withstand such high usage.

I've heard some AI self-driving car pundits say that even if the maintenance needs rise, so what, since you can just tell the AI self-driving car to go to the maintenance shop to get repaired. Maybe we'll have maintenance shops that work late at night, and our AI self-driving cars will all drive to those maintenance places while we sleep. Notably, we're once again cutting out some of the available time to use the AI self-driving car, and so we need to keep in mind that we are reducing the use of the resource. It's not going to be non-stop 24×7 anymore, and maybe more like 20×7 if we assume that on the average it needs to be in the shop some number of hours per day (this does not suggest it will happen each day per se, but that it might be in the shop for an entire day and so we are apportioning that over the course of a week).

Let's assume that we will go along with the pundits and agree that having the AI self-driving car go to the shop, on its own, relieves the human owner of the burden of dealing with the maintenance. What about the cost of this maintenance? You can imagine that if your AI self-driving car is continually going to the shop, the costs of owning and maintaining the car is going to go up, quite a bit.

Not only is the cost of maintenance going to rise, presumably a lot, we can make the assumption that the number of miles put on the car is going to go up, exponentially. This also tends to imply that the value of the car will drop, fast, as it rapidly becomes a more used car. Today, we all realize that the moment you drive a car off the lot after buying it that the value immediately drops. Once you've got your non-stop 24×7 AI self-driving car going for a few months, imagine how much value it will have lost.

We also need to consider the fuel costs. If the AI self-driving car uses gasoline, this non-stop 24×7 use will have a voracious appetite for gasoline. Your fuel costs are going to go through the roof. What impact will this have on the price of gasoline? If the demand for gasoline rises due to the AI self-driving cars on the road, is there even sufficient supply available to meet the demand. Will the price of gasoline go up, since it will be in such high demand?

I know that some of you will say that we should be getting rid of our reliance on gasoline and that AI self-driving cars should be electric instead. Generally, yes, we'll likely be seeing that AI self-driving cars are going to go the electric route. You then need to add the cost of electricity for charging these cars. And, the length of time to charge a car will need to be factored into this, thus again reducing the amount of available usage time of the AI self-driving car.

Hidden Bugs Could Surface with 24×7 Self-Driving Car Use

Another interesting aspect of the non-stop 24×7 approach involves the potential for encountering bugs or errors in the AI systems of the AI self-driving car. Allow me to explain.

You might be assuming that the AI self-driving car is going to work perfectly, other than those annoying physical breakdowns that might occur such as the carburetor or the brakes going bad. I hope you are sitting down when I mention that the AI systems driving the car are not going to be 100% perfect. There is a chance that there will be errors or bugs in the AI system.

If the AI self-driving car wasn't driving around much, the errors or bugs might not either be encountered or rarely encountered. Once the AI self-driving cars are going non-stop 24×7, the odds rise that at some point a hidden bug or error will be invoked. This means that the AI self-driving car might do something wacky, or untoward, or have other ill-suited behavior. The consequences can range from nominal to severely adverse (including crashing or getting into an accident).

By-and-large, the AI self-driving cars will have Over-The-Air (OTA) capabilities, meaning that bug fixes can be pushed down into the AI self-driving car. This though is somewhat misleading because first we need to know that the bug or error exists, and when it first arises it could happen unexpectedly and seemingly randomly until traced to its origins. There's the time needed for the auto maker or tech firm to craft a fix. There's the downtime of the AI self-driving car as it is waiting to get the fix (if its safest to stop the usage until a fix is available), and the downtime when it actually gets the OTA update. There's also the chances that once it gets the OTA update, it might intermingle with some other aspect of the car that creates other new issues.

With the non-stop 24×7 AI self-driving car being on the road so much, we can expect that breakdowns while on the road will rise. Your AI self-driving car is going through the drive-thru at McDonald's for you and was intended to head back to your home to deliver the meal to you. Unfortunately, due to the non-stop usage that's been happening for months on end, all of a sudden your AI self-driving car breaks down at the McDonald's window. You need to get a tow of your AI self-driving car to a maintenance facility.

Let's therefore add the cost of towing to our basket of costs for the non-stop AI self-driving car. Plus, since we are saying that the AI self-driving car will be going 24×7, your AI self-driving car might breakdown at 3 a.m. and need a tow at that time. This could be expensive to get a tow at oddball times of the day or night. You might say, well, just let the AI self-driving car sit wherever it is until the normal tow time arrives, but this assumes that your AI self-driving car has not broken down in the middle of a road and blocking traffic, or that you otherwise need to get it back into service as soon as you can.

I'll further up the ante by pointing out that the non-stop 24×7 AI self-driving car is going to get into accidents more frequently due to the 24×7 usage. There are some AI self-driving car pundits that insist we're going to have "zero fatalities" once we have AI self-driving cars, implying there won't be any accidents at all. Nonsense. First, we are going to have a mixture of human driven cars and AI self-driving cars for the foreseeable future. Therefore, we will have accidents involving both human driven cars and AI self-driving cars. It is inevitable. Second, an AI self-driving car is not a tank, in the sense that if some kid tosses a rock off an overpass and it hits an AI self-driving car, the AI self-driving car is going to suffer damage.

The rise in accidents involving AI self-driving cars that are non-stop 24×7 will increase the need for the AI self-driving cars to be in the maintenance and repair shop, and thus increase the amount of downtime of the AI self-driving car. Once again, it will raise the costs of owning an AI self-driving car.

Take a macroscopic view and consider what these non-stop 24×7 AI self-driving cars will do to our transportation infrastructure. Our roads are barely tolerable today in terms of potholes and other roadway surface and structure issues. With say 200 million AI self-driving cars driving all over the place, non-stop, 24×7, you can bet it will undermine the roads and we as a society will need to spend more money on our transportation infrastructure. You can take that cost and apportion it to all of the car owners and impute that their ownership has a higher cost due to covering our roadway system for this increased usage.

By now, I hope you are convinced that the idyllic world of non-stop 24×7 AI self-driving cars is filled with lots of rubber-meets-the-road pitfalls and added costs. There isn't such a thing as a free lunch.

Speaking of costs, we don't yet know what the cost of a true AI self-driving car is going to be. Let's assume it is going to at least at the start be costlier than conventional cars. The question then arises as to who can afford these fancy, expensive AI self-driving cars. Besides the purchase cost, let's pile on top the added costs due to the increased maintenance and repairs, the added fuel costs, and so on. The affordability would seem to exceed that of the average person to buy such a car. Will then AI self-driving cars become a rich person's vehicle and not be available for the masses. Will these create ill-will and a sense of elitism about AI self-driving cars.

There's another way around this, namely that people will buy an AI self-driving car for both their own needs and to have a ridesharing revenue generating resource (often referred to as Metered Access to Shared Cars or MASC).

This means that a potential buyer of an AI self-driving car might be able to get a loan to cover the cost of the AI self-driving car, since it will essentially pay for itself over time. This raises other issues such as changes in accounting rules for how we treat these revenue generating cars for tax purposes and as a capital investment. The average person might end-up forming a company to help purchase their revenue generating AI self-driving car, rather than making the purchase as an individual. There are open questions about how the ridesharing will be arranged, such as via using a conventional service like an Uber or Lyft, or maybe via social media such as Facebook or Twitter. Time will tell.

Providing your AI self-driving car as a ridesharing capability will aid in the affordability factor, and it will be a means to fill-up the 24×7 of intended non-stop usage. While you are at work, you rideshare out your AI self-driving car. While you are sleeping, you rideshare out your AI self-driving car. This though does begin to put a pinch on your desire to have your AI self-driving car available at your beck and call.

Suppose you've sent it along to do a ride for someone headed to the airport, and meanwhile you suddenly have your spleen burst and want to have your AI self-driving car urgently drive you over to the local emergency room. It will be somewhat tricky to consider how much of the time you want your AI self-driving car doing ridesharing versus being parked and not earning income, but ready immediately for your use.

There are additional ways to also derive revenue from your AI self-driving car. Some believe that AI self-driving car will be outfitted with LED's and displays in them, so that you can watch movies and other entertainment while in the car. It seems logical to assume that we'll all be spending lots of time in our AI self-driving cars and doing so with no need to pay attention to the road, thus we'll want to be entertained. Some even think that we'll want to make classrooms inside of our AI self-driving cars, using our in-car time by taking online classes and earning college credits or getting certifications, doing so a few hours at a time on our daily commutes to work.

This in-car extravaganza of online displays provides an opportunity for having ads shown to us. Therefore, besides renting out your AI self-driving car via ridesharing, you might also be willing to have ad placement for whatever is being shown inside your AI self-driving car to occupants that are using the AI self-driving car. We'll have to see whether occupants are willing to tolerate this. The good news is that it might mean that the ridesharing cost to the occupants possibly goes down, as long as they are willing to endure tons of ads. The ad revenue comes to you, the owner of that expensive AI self-driving car and can offset all of those ongoing costs for keeping the machine running.

The emergence of true Level 5 self-driving cars will undoubtedly convince us to use our AI self-driving cars on a non-stop 24×7 basis. It sounds logical. It seems smart. Unlock the hidden potential that exists today in conventional cars and remains untapped. As mentioned, the benefits of having a 24×7 advanced car seem relatively apparent, while the added costs and downsides are rarely pointed out. I am not casting aspersions on the notion of the non-stop 24×7 AI self-driving car. Just trying to make sure we all have a realistic understanding of what's to come next. And, with that realization, start planning to ensure that we can really achieve the non-stop quest and not get stopped along the way there.

CHAPTER 13

HUMAN LIFE SPANS

AND SELF-DRIVING CARS

CHAPTER 13

HUMAN LIFE SPANS
AND SELF-DRIVING CARS

What is the secret to achieving old age?

Jeanne Calment, having lived to the age of 122, had attributed her longevity to her diet which was rich in olive oil. Sarah DeRemer Knauss, an American supercentenarian, lived 119 years and credited her longevity to the aspect that she didn't let things in life upset her. Indeed, when she first had learned that she had become verified as longest known living person in modern history (at that point in time), she apparently said "so what?" Or, you might find of interest the case of Susannah Jones, she happily consumed four strips of bacon for breakfast each morning, which was included with her scrambled eggs and grits, and was known to eat bacon throughout each day – she lived 116 years.

Does this mean that if you are desirous of reaching a ripe old age that you should rush out to buy lots of olive oil and bacon, along with adjusting your perspective about life to keep from getting upset? Well, maybe. I can't say for sure that this won't help you, but nor can we say with any certainty that it will help you to make it into your hundreds.

One acrimonious debate about old age is whether you are born with the ability to reach it or whether it is your environment that can produce it. Some say that it has to do with DNA. Your DNA either has some kind of longevity gene or it does not. If you weren't born with it, you are out of luck in terms of trying to reach the topmost ages. Sorry to say. Of course, merely being born with the proclivity doesn't guarantee it will bear out. You could perish in an earthquake, get hit by a car, or be involved in a war and die that way.

In this nature versus nurture debate, some would argue that your environment is the primary influencer for successfully reaching old age. If you live in a place that provides a suitable climate, if you live nearby those that can help care for you when you get aged, if you have medical assistance that can apply the latest life extending care, under these conditions you have a chance of achieving older age. Someone that might have a perfectly nature-designed old-age DNA can be readily wiped out sooner by living in a place and time that does not foster living to an older age.

Maybe both nature and nurture intertwine such that we cannot separate one factor from the other. Perhaps the ultimate environment for aiding aging can keep anyone going, regardless if their genes were suitable per se. The person with super aging DNA maybe can tolerate an environment not quite as suitable and still make it. I'd guess this debate will continue for quite some time to come.

Let's shift the debate to another equally interesting question, namely whether there is a limit to how old someone can become? For this question, I'm sure that most of us would say that yes, there has to be a limit. It seems unimaginable that you could just keep living and living and living. Wouldn't the human body just plain wear out? We've seen many science fiction movies where they take someone's brain and place it into another human's body, a younger body, in order to achieve a kind of immortality.

A recent study reported in Science magazine postulated that maybe we can keep doing things in our environment that can extend old age. Perhaps there is no limit per se. Upon analyzing various mortality rates, they suggested that once you reach the age of 105 (yes, I think you will!), the mathematically imputed probability of death seems to stop increasing. One interpretation is that we have not yet reached a limit and we have thus yet to know what the limit is. This does not necessarily mean that life is going to be limitless in aging, but just that we haven't found the end point as yet.

Others that have studied aging find this to be a bit off-target in terms of how the study was conducted and the kinds of interpretations to be made of it. First, trying to assert that there's no upper limit seems quite speculative and not really the spirit of the data that was collected and assessed. Second, if suppose that one person can live to the age of 140, would that be construed that we all have a chance of doing so? In other words, the statistical anomaly of someone out of the billions of people on this planet that happens to make it to some incredible older age should not be falsely used to suggest we all can, or that even many of us can, or even that a few can. It might be a lighting strike kind of occurrence.

However this old age debate ends-up faring, the general rule-of-thumb seems to be that for most of us, we can live to some ripe older age by eating right, watching our health, taking less risks, keep our bodies in shape, and keep our minds in shape. This is not the secret formula to get you to the hundreds, and instead the traditional advice about how to keep going to some kind of older age. Plus, as per the famous quote by Theodore Roosevelt, old is age is like anything else, to make a success of it, you've got to start young. Presumably, if when younger you eat poorly, don't watch your health, take high risks, don't keep your body in shape, and don't keep your mind sharp, trying to suddenly change your ways at a later age might be too late. The damage was already done, some say.

What does this have to do with AI self-driving cars?

At the Cybernetic AI Self-Driving Car Institute, we are developing AI systems for self-driving cars and also keenly interested in how self-driving cars will be used by society.

Here's a thought provoking assertion: AI self-driving cars will help to maximize human life spans.

I've debated this topic at some industry conferences and thought you'd like to know about it. There are already assertions that AI self-driving cars will reduce the number of car related deaths, which is considered one of the largest benefits to society for the advent of self-driving cars. I agree that someday it is likely that AI self-driving cars will reduce the number of car related deaths, but I also claim that it is many years into the future and that for the foreseeable future it won't materially impact the number of car related deaths. Indeed, I argue that this whole idea of "zero fatalities" is a gimmick and misleading or stated by those that are perhaps misinformed on the matter.

Even if the advent of AI self-driving cars eliminated all car related deaths, you need to realize that the number of car related deaths per year in the United States is about 40,000. There are about 325 million people in the United States. As such, though every life is precious, the saving of 40,000 lives out of a population of 325 million is important but not something that will cure all deaths from happening. There are an estimated 650,000 deaths each year in the U.S. due to heart disease, and another 600,000 deaths due to cancer. In theory, if we were only looking at number of deaths as a metric, we would say that we should take all the money spent toward AI self-driving cars and put it toward curing heart disease and cancer, since that has a much higher death rate than car related deaths.

The point here is that the AI self-driving car emergence will not presumably alter the likelihood of achieving older age by the act of reducing or eliminating deaths in the population. That's not going to move the needle on the old age achievement scale.

What then might the AI self-driving car be able to do to advance our ages?

One aspect that is touted about AI self-driving cars is that it will increase the mobility of humans. There are some that say we are going to become a mobility-as-an-economy type of society. With the access to 24x7 car transportation and an electronic chauffeur that will drive you wherever you want to go, it will mean that people today that aren't readily mobile can become mobile. Kids that can't drive today will be able to use an AI self-driving car to get them to school or to the playground or wherever they need to go. The elderly that no longer are licensed to drive will be able to get out of their homes and no longer be homebound, doing so by making use of AI self-driving cars.

So, we can make the claim that via the use of more prevalent mobility, it could allow those that are older to be able to more readily visit with say medical advisers and ensure that their healthcare is being taken care of. Need a trip to the local hospital? In today's terms, it might be logistically prohibitive for the homebound elder to make such a trip. In contrast, presumably with ease they will be able to call forth an AI self-driving car that can give them a lift to the nearby medical care facility.

Healthcare can also more readily come to them, including having clinicians that go around in AI self-driving cars and can visit with those that need medical assistance. If you are willing to believe that having timely medical care is an important factor in achieving and maintaining older age, the AI self-driving car can be a catalyst for that to occur.

Another case of how an AI self-driving car might contribute to the aging process in terms of prolonging life might be due to increase access to other humans and presumably gaining greater mental stimulation and joy in life. Want to visit your grandchildren? Rather than having to arrange for some convoluted logistics, you just get the AI self-driving car to take you to them. Again, the reduced friction in mobility, some would say it is frictionless (I think though that's a tad over-the-top), allows for trying to keep both body and mind in shape.

Some say that isolation tends to lead to early deaths. AI self-driving cars have the potential for increasing socialization and reducing isolation. This is achieved by the ease of mobility. In addition, while in an AI self-driving car, it is predicted that AI self-driving cars will have all sorts of electronic communication capabilities, and during a journey you can be doing all kinds of Skype-like communication with others. Thus, even if in an AI self-driving car and all alone in doing so, you can actually be interacting with others during a driving trip.

Another factor might be physical fitness. If you are at home and isolated, you might not be inspired to do physical fitness. Admittedly there are more and more in-the-home treadmills and bikes that will allow you to virtually interact with others across the globe, but this still doesn't seem to be as meaningful and motivating as doing so in-person. With an AI self-driving car, you could readily get to some location whereby physical fitness with others is able to take place in-person. It might be to get you to the yoga shop or the local gym.

Food and nutrition seem to be a factor in extending life. Once again, the mobility aspects of the AI self-driving car can assist. We already have lots of ridesharing like services emerging today that will bring food to your home. The emergence of AI self-driving cars is going to certainly expand that capability. The so-called "boxes on wheels" will be food delivery vehicles that are being operated as AI self-driving cars. The ease of getting food delivered to your home will be simplified.

This all seems pretty good and an encouragement that AI self-driving cars might have another significant benefit to society, namely extending our life spans. It is perhaps an indirect mechanism rather than a direct mechanism. I say this because the AI self-driving car itself is not per se extending life. It is the consequences of what the AI self-driving car can provide as capabilities that ties into the factors that presumably lead to longer lives. I mention this because sometimes someone will argue that it is "unfair" to suggest that the AI self-driving car is extending our life spans – but it isn't a pill that you swallow, it isn't something you wear on your back like a special kind of cloak. Yes, I agree, it's what the AI self-driving car can otherwise do that counts here.

As with anything that can be a benefit, the odds are that there will be potential unintended adverse consequences too. The AI self-driving car could actually become a life limiter, rather than a life extender.

Suppose that the advent of AI self-driving cars allows people to take greater risks by having the AI self-driving car drive them to cliff diving or to parachute jumping. You could use the mobility for purposes that put you at greater risk. Maybe you have the self-driving car bring you fatty foods every day to home and to work. Perhaps you use the self-driving car to avoid having to contend with visitors by never being at home? You might even become addicted to your AI self-driving car, which is unlikely to aid in your potential quest for longevity.

You've likely seen the famous sigmoid graph that shows the typical mortality rate for humans. It's a kind of "S" curve that starts up, then stays at a relatively constant rate of increase, and then tails off at the end. Benjamin Gompertz was the famous mathematician that is most known as the formulator of the "law of mortality" and for which he asserted that the human rate of death is related to age as a sigmoid function. A variant is the Gompertz-Makeham law that includes the sum of age-independent components.

Is there perhaps no true ceiling for human aging? Is the sky the limit? Or, do we all have a stamped on us a perishable by date X that we don't even know is there?

Gompertz's indication that resistance to death decreases as the years increase might either be an immutable law of nature, or maybe it is something that we can defy or at least extend. If you are looking for more reasons to want to have AI self-driving cars, one could be that it might aid our societal efforts to maximize our life spans. Some might see this as a bit of a stretch and be upset that the AI self-driving car itself is not really doing this, and instead it is the consequence of what the AI self-driving car can possibly provide. Either way, its certainly an intriguing notion and one that might help us all as we struggle to get AI self-driving cars into suitable shape for aiding society. The pain along the way might be worth the advantages it can provide once we get there. I'll see you on the other side of 150 years of age.

APPENDIX

APPENDIX A
TEACHING WITH THIS MATERIAL

The material in this book can be readily used either as a supplemental to other content for a class, or it can also be used as a core set of textbook material for a specialized class. Classes where this material is most likely used include any classes at the college or university level that want to augment the class by offering thought provoking and educational essays about AI and self-driving cars.

In particular, here are some aspects for class use:

o   Computer Science. Studying AI, autonomous vehicles, etc.

o   Business. Exploring technology and it adoption for business.

o   Sociology. Sociological views on the adoption and advancement of technology.

Specialized classes at the undergraduate and graduate level can also make use of this material.

For each chapter, consider whether you think the chapter provides material relevant to your course topic. There is plenty of opportunity to get the students thinking about the topic and force them to decide whether they agree or disagree with the points offered and positions taken. I would also encourage you to have the students do additional research beyond the chapter material presented (I provide next some suggested assignments they can do).

RESEARCH ASSIGNMENTS ON THESE TOPICS

Your students can find background material on these topics, doing so in various business and technical publications. I list below the top ranked AI related journals. For business publications, I would suggest the usual culprits such as the Harvard Business Review, Forbes, Fortune, WSJ, and the like.

Here are some suggestions of homework or projects that you could assign to students:

a) <u>Assignment for foundational AI research topic</u>: Research and prepare a paper and a presentation on a specific aspect of Deep AI, Machine Learning, ANN, etc. The paper should cite at least 3 reputable sources. Compare and contrast to what has been stated in this book.

b) <u>Assignment for the Self-Driving Car topic</u>: Research and prepare a paper and Self-Driving Cars. Cite at least 3 reputable sources and analyze the characterizations. Compare and contrast to what has been stated in this book.

c) <u>Assignment for a Business topic</u>: Research and prepare a paper and a presentation on businesses and advanced technology. What is hot, and what is not? Cite at least 3 reputable sources. Compare and contrast to the depictions in this book.

d) <u>Assignment to do a Startup:</u> Have the students prepare a paper about how they might startup a business in this realm. They must submit a sound Business Plan for the startup. They could also be asked to present their Business Plan and so should also have a presentation deck to coincide with it.

You can certainly adjust the aforementioned assignments to fit to your particular needs and the class structure. You'll notice that I ask for 3 reputable cited sources for the paper writing based assignments. I usually steer students toward "reputable" publications, since otherwise they will cite some oddball source that has no credentials other than that they happened to write something and post it onto the Internet. You can define "reputable" in whatever way you prefer, for example some faculty think Wikipedia is not reputable while others believe it is reputable and allow students to cite it.

The reason that I usually ask for at least 3 citations is that if the student only does one or two citations they usually settle on whatever they happened to find the fastest. By requiring three citations, it usually seems to force them to look around, explore, and end-up probably finding five or more, and then whittling it down to 3 that they will actually use.

I have not specified the length of their papers, and leave that to you to tell the students what you prefer. For each of those assignments, you could end-up with a short one to two pager, or you could do a dissertation length paper. Base the length on whatever best fits for your class, and the credit amount of the assignment within the context of the other grading metrics you'll be using for the class.

I mention in the assignments that they are to do a paper and prepare a presentation. I usually try to get students to present their work. This is a good practice for what they will do in the business world. Most of the time, they will be required to prepare an analysis and present it. If you don't have the class time or inclination to have the students present, then you can of course cut out the aspect of them putting together a presentation.

If you want to point students toward highly ranked journals in AI, here's a list of the top journals as reported by *various citation counts sources* (this list changes year to year):

o   Communications of the ACM

o   Artificial Intelligence

o   Cognitive Science

o   IEEE Transactions on Pattern Analysis and Machine Intelligence

o   Foundations and Trends in Machine Learning

o   Journal of Memory and Language

o   Cognitive Psychology

o   Neural Networks

o   IEEE Transactions on Neural Networks and Learning Systems

o   IEEE Intelligent Systems

o   Knowledge-based Systems

GUIDE TO USING THE CHAPTERS

For each of the chapters, I provide next some various ways to use the chapter material. You can assign the tasks as individual homework assignments, or the tasks can be used with team projects for the class. You can easily layout a series of assignments, such as indicating that the students are to do item "a" below for say Chapter 1, then "b" for the next chapter of the book, and so on.

a) What is the main point of the chapter and describe in your own words the significance of the topic,

b) Identify at least two aspects in the chapter that you agree with, and support your concurrence by providing at least one other outside researched item as support; make sure to explain your basis for disagreeing with the aspects,

c) Identify at least two aspects in the chapter that you disagree with, and support your disagreement by providing at least one other outside researched item as support; make sure to explain your basis for disagreeing with the aspects,

d) Find an aspect that was not covered in the chapter, doing so by conducting outside research, and then explain how that aspect ties into the chapter and what significance it brings to the topic,

e) Interview a specialist in industry about the topic of the chapter, collect from them their thoughts and opinions, and readdress the chapter by citing your source and how they compared and contrasted to the material,

f) Interview a relevant academic professor or researcher in a college or university about the topic of the chapter, collect from them their thoughts and opinions, and readdress the chapter by citing your source and how they compared and contrasted to the material,

g) Try to update a chapter by finding out the latest on the topic, and ascertain whether the issue or topic has now been solved or whether it is still being addressed, explain what you come up with.

The above are all ways in which you can get the students of your class involved in considering the material of a given chapter. You could mix things up by having one of those above assignments per each week, covering the chapters over the course of the semester or quarter.

As a reminder, here are the chapters of the book and you can select whichever chapters you find most valued for your particular class:

Companion Book By This Author

Advances in AI and Autonomous Vehicles: Cybernetic Self-Driving Cars

*Practical Advances in Artificial Intelligence (AI)
and Machine Learning*
by
Dr. Lance B. Eliot, MBA, PhD

This title is available via Amazon and other book sellers

Companion Book By This Author

Self-Driving Cars:
"The Mother of All AI Projects"

by Dr. Lance B. Eliot, MBA, PhD

This title is available via Amazon and other book sellers

<u>Companion Book By This Author</u>

Innovation and Thought Leadership on Self-Driving Driverless Cars

by Dr. Lance B. Eliot, MBA, PhD

<u>Chapter Title</u>

This title is available via Amazon and other book sellers

Companion Book By This Author

New Advances in AI Autonomous Driverless Cars Self-Driving Cars

by Dr. Lance B. Eliot, MBA, PhD

<u>Chapter Title</u>

This title is available via Amazon and other book sellers

Companion Book By This Author

Introduction to
Driverless Self-Driving Cars

by Dr. Lance B. Eliot, MBA, PhD

This title is available via Amazon and other book sellers

Companion Book By This Author
Autonomous Vehicle Driverless Self-Driving Cars and Artificial Intelligence
by Dr. Lance B. Eliot, MBA, PhD

Chapter Title

This title is available via Amazon and other book sellers

<u>Companion Book By This Author</u>

Transformative Artificial Intelligence Driverless Self-Driving Cars

by Dr. Lance B. Eliot, MBA, PhD

<u>Chapter Title</u>

This title is available via Amazon and other book sellers

Companion Book By This Author

Disruptive Artificial Intelligence and Driverless Self-Driving Cars

by Dr. Lance B. Eliot, MBA, PhD

Chapter Title

1 Eliot Framework for AI Self-Driving Cars

2 Maneuverability and Self-Driving Cars

3 Common Sense Reasoning and Self-Driving Cars

4 Cognition Timing and Self-Driving Cars

5 Speed Limits and Self-Driving Vehicles

6 Human Back-up Drivers and Self-Driving Cars

7 Forensic Analysis Uber and Self-Driving Cars

8 Power Consumption and Self-Driving Cars

9 Road Rage and Self-Driving Cars

10 Conspiracy Theories and Self-Driving Cars

11 Fear Landscape and Self-Driving Cars

12 Pre-Mortem and Self-Driving Cars

13 Kits and Self-Driving Cars

This title is available via Amazon and other book sellers

Companion Book By This Author

State-of-the-Art
AI Driverless Self-Driving Cars

by Dr. Lance B. Eliot, MBA, PhD

This title is available via Amazon and other book sellers

Companion Book By This Author

Top Trends in
AI Self-Driving Cars

by Dr. Lance B. Eliot, MBA, PhD

Chapter Title

This title is available via Amazon and other book sellers

ABOUT THE AUTHOR

Dr. Lance B. Eliot, MBA, PhD is the CEO of Techbruim, Inc. and Executive Director of the Cybernetic Self-Driving Car Institute, and has over twenty years of industry experience including serving as a corporate officer in a billion dollar firm and was a partner in a major executive services firm. He is also a serial entrepreneur having founded, ran, and sold several high-tech related businesses. He previously hosted the popular radio show *Technotrends* that was also available on American Airlines flights via their in-flight audio program. Author or co-author of a dozen books and over 400 articles, he has made appearances on CNN, and has been a frequent speaker at industry conferences.

A former professor at the University of Southern California (USC), he founded and led an innovative research lab on Artificial Intelligence in Business. Known as the "AI Insider" his writings on AI advances and trends has been widely read and cited. He also previously served on the faculty of the University of California Los Angeles (UCLA), and was a visiting professor at other major universities. He was elected to the International Board of the Society for Information Management (SIM), a prestigious association of over 3,000 high-tech executives worldwide.

He has performed extensive community service, including serving as Senior Science Adviser to the Vice Chair of the Congressional Committee on Science & Technology. He has served on the Board of the OC Science & Engineering Fair (OCSEF), where he is also has been a Grand Sweepstakes judge, and likewise served as a judge for the Intel International SEF (ISEF). He served as the Vice Chair of the Association for Computing Machinery (ACM) Chapter, a prestigious association of computer scientists. Dr. Eliot has been a shark tank judge for the USC Mark Stevens Center for Innovation on start-up pitch competitions, and served as a mentor for several incubators and accelerators in Silicon Valley and Silicon Beach. He served on several Boards and Committees at USC, including having served on the Marshall Alumni Association (MAA) Board in Southern California.

Dr. Eliot holds a PhD from USC, MBA, and Bachelor's in Computer Science, and earned the CDP, CCP, CSP, CDE, and CISA certifications. Born and raised in Southern California, and having traveled and lived internationally, he enjoys scuba diving, surfing, and sailing.

ADDENDUM

AI Innovations and Self-Driving Cars

Practical Advances in Artificial Intelligence (AI) and Machine Learning

By

Dr. Lance B. Eliot, MBA, PhD

———

For supplemental materials of this book, visit:

www.ai-selfdriving-cars.guru

For special orders of this book, contact:

LBE Press Publishing

Email: LBE.Press.Publishing@gmail.com

www.ingramcontent.com/pod-product-compliance
Lightning Source LLC
Chambersburg PA
CBHW051235050326
40689CB00007B/926

* 9 7 8 0 6 9 2 1 6 1 7 5 3 *